Yearning for the seemingly impossible is the path to human progress.

- Bryant H. McGill

To Ollie and Lucy,

My eternal hope is that you, and the generations that follow you, live in a world that embraces the *collective intelligence* of the human race. The kind of society that promotes individual freedoms, creativity, innovation, and entrepreneurial spirit.

It is times such as these that mark when humanity makes the most impressive leaps forward.

Unfortunately, such environments are not pre-ordained. In fact, the darkest periods in human history correlate with the opposite.

Unlike in previous eras, the challenges the human race face today are multiple and loom far more prominent than ever. However, I am confident that if we can come together, co-operate, collaborate, and innovate, we will once again do what humans do best: overcome the seemingly impossible.

With Special Thanks

It's only when you write a book that you see the value and importance of an acknowledgments section.

A list of names that likely mean nothing to most readers, but without whose input and inspiration the book would never even have got off the ground.

In this regard, and in my case, thanks have to go out to hundreds of people. Some I have never met, but their thoughts and works have profoundly affected my own. There are also those around me who have endured me talking about the topic of this book for years: and always remained supportive.

The podcast I host, *Transitional Matters*, has also been a fertile discussion ground, with conversations that both supported and challenged my thoughts.

Beyond this, thanks must go to three people who have shaped the way I think more than any others. My late mother, Frances Marshall, as well as Lesley Bell, and Danie Strydom.

Thank you.

Contents

Preface

∞

Looking back, I can see that this topic has had a natural hold on me for most of my life.

From an early age, there was an inborn curiosity to understand the big picture and with it, the links between how we see the world and the trends and transitions going on in it.

Time is always on the move. Yet we get to see just a glimpse of it through our own eyes.

As a young boy, I was fortunate to grow up in the stunning countryside of North Wales. Not only did this afford me an uncommon level of freedom, but also an eerie link to the past.

Those who have had the pleasure of visiting this lush green land will have noticed that most of the roads twist and turn at every opportunity.

But now and again, you come across a road that stands out. A road that is almost pinned straight, bending only where absolutely necessary. These were clearly built by very different builders.

Whether true or not, I was told as a boy of seven or eight that these straight roads were the lasting marks of Roman occupation some two thousand years before. Apparently, these roads not only significantly reduced the Roman commute, but also curbed the chances of crime taking place, too, with far fewer bends and corners for bandits and robbers to lurk.

But there was a question I could not shake. A question that would lay dormant for years.

For all their know-how and technological prowess, how could such an advanced civilization have collapsed and disappeared? As a boy, it didn't seem to make sense.

I was yet to appreciate that on a long enough time scale, there was an almost continuous rise and fall of global powers, with culture and innovation at its heart.

In short, when a country ceases to remain the leading innovative nation, its power and voice at the table of the global order fade too. But when a civilization ceases to retain its essential innovative ability? It falls.

This has happened time and time again. We could trace this through the ancient empires, republics, and kingdoms, as well as the more modern ones, such as the passing of the baton from the Dutch Republic, the British Empire, and then to the United States of America.

In this book, I want to show you a world below the noise of the daily news feed. Here, at this level, it's a far slower changing world. A world where we talk about immensely compelling trends, megatrends, and critical points of transition that play out over decades, not days.

Unfortunately, this world remains hidden from most of society.

These trends and megatrends hold not only the fate of ancient empires but also, in our time, the fate of the country likely to hold the title of superpower, or even hyperpower, in the future.

Trends speak of which jobs will remain in demand and what skill sets will fall by the wayside. Trends show where people will likely have to migrate from and to as the climate continues to change. And trends also show how societal attitudes, morals, values, and beliefs could change over time too.

My natural curiosity to see the bigger picture only grew over the years. It would take a significant step forward in 2015 when I completed my MSc research focusing on the growing field of behavioural economics and more broadly, behavioural science: the science of how we make decisions.

Here, I started to see the empirical link between the effects of uncertainty and our natural risk aversion response at such times. In other words, as things get uncertain, we step off the gas.

While this might sound normal – its consequences can be profound. This is especially true when we consider that we are hardwired to experience loss (and even the anticipation of loss) more powerfully than we experience equivalent gains.

The result is as uncertainty rises we cling to the familiar – the status quo.

A millennia ago, when uncertainty arose, it was a credible signal that we should become more cautious. Wild animals could be lurking – and sticking to the paths you knew could be a lifesaving move.

But the modern world is very different.

Today, we could argue that sticking to the status quo is more dangerous than embracing change. Uncertainty and fears today spring from a different place than in times gone by.

To see and understand change today, I suggest we view it from as many angles as possible. We need to step back from being the hyper-specialists in a single domain and view it from a higher plane.

This includes a better understanding of how change affects us and our decision-making.

As a futurist and behavioural scientist, I am privileged to put much of this into my work as Head of Global Investment Strategy for Dragon Investment Managers. A role where understating the big-picture is vital to doing a good job and steering investment portfolios in the right direction.

From my observations, while many people have a keen eye on a specific area, say demographics, resource scarcity, debt cycles, climate change, or technological advances, they miss the vital step of standing back and seeing how it is all linked.

In complex environments such as the world we live in, rarely does anything happen in isolation.

If we are to get better at seeing change at the global scale, we must develop an appreciation for the feedback loops between the different layers of the world around us.

Change is not a smooth, linear process, and not everything changes at the same time and pace. This fact alone causes imbalances and sits at the core of disruption.

In our journey together, we'll look at how to join all the dots. In doing this, I make no apologies for reasonable simplification. This book is not an academic textbook; quite the opposite, it's a book full of what I hope you will find is an insight-yielding narrative.

In my view, capturing the essence of the big picture is often more important than understanding the minutiae of one single corner but remaining blind to the rest. The old saying 'you can't see the forest for the trees' is perhaps apt in this regard.

As you lengthen the time that you think over and start to step back from the noise, I hope and expect there will be a naturally growing level of curiosity and wonder about what goes on around us. An ever-changing world calls for an ever-present student. We all have more to learn, more to understand, and more to see. In the coming decades, I fundamentally believe that curiosity will be a superpower.

Therefore, I encourage you to stand back from events, question what you think you know, and instead see how things move over extended periods of time.

Along the way, I hope you come to a deep-seated sense of optimism rooted in what can only be described as the immense creative ability of the human race to innovate and adapt when faced with seemingly impossible situations. This book is nothing more than an attempt to help you know where to look.

Chris Marshall

July 2022

Introduction

∞

Whichever way you look at it, the world has changed – dramatically – and the changes coming aren't likely to slow in pace or decrease in magnitude either.

If anything, they're expected to speed up and even expand.

There's an issue with that.

With change comes uncertainty, fear, and anxiety, and the tendency to cling to the status quo – perhaps the last thing we want to do in a fast-changing world.

This book's core aim is to help you better understand change. To deepen your understanding of where change comes from and the common patterns through which it plays out.

Unfortunately, as a society, we don't spend much time thinking about change at the big-picture level. However, without a framework and basic understanding of how change plays out, it's all too easy for the future to become a place of fear that we run from – a place that seems incomprehensible, where we don't understand what's going on.

It's no secret that when we feel heightened levels of uncertainty, we are more likely to become closed-minded and myopically focused – rather than looking up and seeing the big picture. At the same time, our creative outlook fades away. The familiar, the known, and the comfortable become more appealing, and we become less adaptable. We become less curious.

Let's be clear, humanity has many challenges ahead.

Climate change poses the greatest threat the human race has ever had to overcome. But it's far from the only one.

Despite this, I'm optimistic that we can overcome these challenges, but my optimism comes with a caveat.

We must bring our best selves to the game. That means not only being more creative and open-minded, but more adaptable, flexible, and ultimately more co-operative. To get there, we must first remove the fear of change, which comes from understanding how it occurs around us and how change affects us at an individual level.

At our best, we humans are enviably innovative and adaptable. But when we are increasingly beset with fear and pessimism about the future, we fail to bring the best version of ourselves to the table.

It's your A-game the world needs right now. More than that, you need your A-game to thrive in a world of rapid change.

Outline

In the first section, we'll start by building a better practical understanding of innovation and change.

Innovation is at the core of human progress, and it follows a pattern – a cycle that we've seen several times since the Industrial Revolution and is likely to continue in the future.

When viewing change from this big picture perspective, many people are met with a kind of 'aha' moment as the things they observe going on around them click into place with far more meaning.

Developing an understanding of how the world changes is only the first step. To truly understand and cope with change, we need to turn our observations inward, too.

Section two deals with just that. It offers a view from within, the importance of optimism, and how information overload and decision fatigue can arise, particularly when the landscape is unfamiliar and unsettling.

If we're going to get better at seeing change, we must get better at filtering out unwanted information and noise that can not only tire us out but also completely throw our thoughts off-course.

Change does not happen in isolation.

Instead, change changes us and everything around us.

During times of change, it's easy to get caught up in unhelpful biases and emotions. It's also at those times we become easily manipulated – something else that we should be aware of.

The book's final section looks at more practical aspects of collective progress, which I suggest rests on our need to restore our faith in humanity as well as the business and economic spheres that operate around us.

We need to work together, collaborate, and find what I call *collective intelligence.*

In previous eras, getting these perspectives wrong brought severe economic consequences and costs. Today, it's different. While the same economic consequences exist, this time, we also require humanity to be at its most productive, most innovative, and most creative if we are to sufficiently adapt to our changing natural environment.

With an understanding of how innovation occurs, how it jumps forwards at certain times, bringing with it new ways of doing things, I'm sure you'll join me in the confidence I have that we can overcome the hurdles that stand before us and even take humanity to the next level – the next golden age.

The seriousness of the challenges that lie ahead is absolute. The very future of humanity rests on getting this right. And we all have a part to play – this starts with understanding change.

Looking back

In the past thirty years alone, we have witnessed the mass adoption of the internet and all that comes with it: emails, social media, the globalisation of data, and the always-on culture. While these things *can* bring humanity many benefits, it has also directly affected our thinking and brains.

It is no coincidence that over this time we have also seen workplace stress move up the ranks. Burnout is no longer just a buzzword reserved for office workaholics. Mindfulness and finding time to retreat from the world has become a pastime for millions. *If I can just stop for a minute and restore calm, then I'll be fine to carry on*, is the mantra of many.

We have become overwhelmed and overloaded with information. Our brains are fried.

But burnout and stress are just the more visible elements of this change.

Less talked about and less observable are the effects this has on our outlook – as well as how far into the future, or past, we now think.

As Herbert Simon put it, 'A wealth of information creates a poverty of attention[i]' (p. 38, 1971).

With minute-by-minute data at our fingertips, we have become addicted to the short term. So much so that many have completely lost sight of larger-scale change. As the world gets faster, we fail to step back, contemplate, and ponder. We are failing to dip below the noise. More than this, we are failing to even notice it's happening.

Most of the time, we can get away with this approach.

That's because most of the time, change is slow enough for us to keep up.

But the assumption that the world only has one speed of change – and that it's a steady one – is a dangerous one to make.

It's much like assuming that the calm-flowing lazy river you find yourself on right now will always be that way, with no rapids or waterfalls at the end.

This book suggests something different; a waterfall that rivals Niagara Falls is just around the corner.

The magnitude of the incoming change has occurred only a handful of times in modern history. It's time to look up.

Why this book?

It has to do with curiosity, it has to do with people wondering what makes something do something, and then to discover that if you try to get answers, that they're related to each other... What we're looking for is how everything works. It's a curiosity to find out what we are and where we are.

– Richard Feynman, Theoretical Physicist, 1918–1988.

The above quote was taken from an interview with the legendary theoretical physicist, Richard Feynman.

Feynman, of course, wasn't explicitly talking about change in the world, but we should note the sentiment and approach to life he points out.

Whoever we are, whatever our jobs, we all have a fundamental need to better understand the world we live in. After all, any long-term decision or commitment we make rests on our understanding of it.

Every fifty to sixty years since the Industrial Revolution, we have seen a new era ushered in through technological breakthrough.

From the age of rail starting in the late 1820s to the age of steel, electricity, and heavy engineering fifty-five years later in 1875.

Since then, we have seen two more waves: the age of oil, automobiles, and mass production, which gathered momentum in the early 1900s, and most recently, the information age beginning when the microchip burst onto the scene at the start of the 1970s.

Fifty years on and we're once again at another turning point.

Several candidates could very well be the root of the next technological wave, including the incorporation of artificial intelligence (AI) and machine learning into everyday tasks.

Beyond this, nanotechnology and the energy transition hold the scope to bring radical transformation.

Each wave of technological revolution has brought tremendous progress for humanity over the longer term.

General prosperity and quality of life have risen.

But in the short term? These changes usher in disruptive and fractious times.

We would do well to understand this seemingly contradictory nature of change and how the short- and long-term effects can be at odds with each other.

Why does this occur?

Our world is geared to the best practices, technology, and infrastructure developed for our current age and paradigm. People's training, skills, and jobs reflect this too.

The advent of paradigm shifting technology is synonymous with the discovery of a *better way* of doing things. A way that has not been thought of before.

Over the long term, this continues to bring increased prosperity.

But new technology, and a better way of doing things, also means that the current set-up is not organised for this new world. It must change. And that change in the short-term results in recessions, debt defaults, inflation and unemployment, and uncertainty, especially when global powers are shifting too.

If we return to the first Industrial Revolution, we learn of the uprising of the Luddites, a group of bandit-like people that felt this force head-on. The new technologies brought about huge uncertainty about the future of their jobs, their lifestyle, and their pay.

Would all their jobs be lost to machines?

In their view, this was highly likely. As their uncertainty turned to fear and anger, they started playing havoc with the new factory owners. They destroyed and vandalized their machines and frames to try and retain the old way of doing things – the status quo.

The Luddites, to be fair, were half right.

In the short term, jobs were lost, lives were disrupted, and wages decreased as their skills were not needed. In the short term, technology held a greater ability to destroy jobs than it did to create them.

But that is merely in the short term.

Take a longer-term view, and the machines have created wealth as new jobs brought about new industries and sectors that were unimaginable at the time. Average wages and general prosperity climbed significantly too.

Today the parallels are all too clear. The rise of AI, machine learning, and robotics threaten to automate vast chunks of work that humans currently do.

It would be all too easy – and naive – to suggest that all will be fine if we look to the long term. But as humans, we must also live in the moment. Now is when our mortgages must be paid and food acquired.

Here lies the deeper purpose of this book. We need to be far more aware of what's happening, so we are not caught off guard.

Getting caught off guard is, at a cognitive level, synonymous with panic and fear – which in turn has a high correlation to turning our backs on change, creativity, and innovation. We also cling to the old way, the status quo.

In the long term, countless jobs will spring up in businesses and industries that we cannot begin to comprehend today. Human progress will continue. We will take more care of the environment and world we live in, have less impact on the land, continue to reduce poverty around the world, and develop medical practices beyond our imagination.

But we must get there first. And that means going through a transitional period.

Section One

The World Around Us

Chapter 1

Uncertainty Abounds

∞

In 2019, researchers at Pew, a nonpartisan research fact-tank, focused on the issues that US teenagers perceived they were facing. The results were nothing less than startling.

At the top of the list of major concerns were anxiety and depression. In fact, some seventy per cent of the adolescents surveyed saw this as a significant concern. More alarmingly, only four per cent of the respondents labelled it as something they consider to be 'no concern at all'.

As I read through the report, anxiety and depression not only topped the list but were also significantly ahead. More visible concerns such as teen pregnancy, bullying, drug addiction, and gangs appeared, in contrast, to be far more minor issues.[1]

Researchers at Pew weren't the only ones highlighting this. In November 2020, a multi-disciplinary group of researchers with backgrounds in psychology, epidemiology, public health, and biostatistical science published their work in the *Journal of Psychiatric Research*. The message was clear. They'd looked at data from 2008 to 2018, and there was a clear trend. Stress and anxiety were increasing, particularly in the younger generations: 'Young people are confronting more potentially anxiety-provoking world events than prior generations, and exposure to such events is now pervasive with access to 24/7 media' (Goodwin et al., 2020, p. 441–446).[2]

Turning to a larger measure of global tension, the Institute for Economics and Peace published an annual report called the Global Peace Index. In what is perhaps the world's leading measure of peacefulness, each year's report is one heck of an undertaking, covering 163 countries and some 99.7 per cent of the world's population.

The fifteenth-anniversary edition, released in 2021, noted that global peacefulness was declining. It wasn't a massive move lower, but it was undoubtedly part of a trend that the researchers had started to notice over the past nine years; each year, the overall level of peacefulness declined just a little more.

New tensions stemming from the Covid-19 pandemic were observed, but also that the gap between the most and least peaceful countries was widening too.

The more conversations I had with people on this topic, the more I realised that this feeling was not exclusive to academic or political circles. The general public had an intuitive sense of growing tensions but couldn't quite put their finger on it.

Uncertainty about the world was rising. While it had not yet transpired to anxiety or outright fear, people commented that their lives were unsettled at some core level. The world they lived in simply felt *different*, as if something had changed and they'd not been told what.

This feeling can be observed on the global stage, too. The standard narrative bombards us with multiple 'causes' from race, gender, and wealth inequality to greedy capitalists sitting back and watching the world burn. But are these the true causes? Or are they mere outcomes from changes at a far deeper level?

We could spend hours arguing where this 'feeling' has shown up the most. But one thing I'm sure we'd ultimately agree on is it's occurring everywhere. Concurrently.

And like it or not, we are being forced to change our ways.

America, being the world's number one economic power – for now at least – holds a natural grip on global attention. Perhaps this hold was increased during the Trump era, with the chosen platform for public announcements being found on social media, particularly President Trump's Twitter account.

The US presidential race in 2020 was, with its almost polar opposites in the form of Trump and Biden, a polarising event and a media godsend that the world couldn't get enough of.

On the night of the election, with a full jug of freshly brewed coffee resting in the kitchen, I was ready to see the US election night through. I'm no US citizen, I live in the UK, but interest and social polarity had reached such a level that I was lined up to speak at a seminar the following morning to discuss the possible market reaction as votes came in.

In such divided times, one thing was not a surprise: the number of voters turning up to cast their ballots and use their voices. These were signs of a truly divided nation, and in many ways, it continues today. The US has around 240 million eligible voters; in 2020, some 158 million of them (sixty-six per cent) turned up. That's the highest level of participation since 1900.

It didn't matter your political views; this election race would not only split the US nation but the global audience, too.

However, there was one thing that both sides could agree on, it was that if the other candidate won, the country would be in trouble. Biden supporters were known as snowflake terrorists to the Trump supporters, who were known as the QAnon crazies.

With the global pandemic in the background, citizens blamed one another for the state of the nation.

Once again, we find the Pew Research Center diving into the heart of the matter – conducting a study on the intense divide that plagued America. One month before the election, roughly every eight out of ten registered voters on both sides said their differences with the other side were about 'core American values'; and roughly nine out of ten worried that a victory by the other would lead to 'lasting harm' to the United States.[3] This fact alone proves that more than half of the majority on both sides of the political spectrum lived in fear over the outcome, regardless of whose candidate won.

When Covid-19 hit, the battle between Republicans and Democrats heightened. Republicans felt President Trump was handling the pandemic pretty well, suspending travel outside the United States and quickening research in coming up with a vaccine.

However, on the flip side, Democrats thought that Donald Trump could have done way more, and add to that, he was to blame for the sky-rocketing death toll that seemed to be growing each day.

Biden supporters felt as if the handling of the coronavirus outbreak in the United States was the central issue when it came to the 2020 elections. Why is this divide growing more evident? Ezra Klein from Pew Research suggests 'Race, religion and ideology now align with partisan identity in ways that they often didn't in eras when the two parties were relatively heterogeneous coalitions' (Dimock & Wike, 2020).[3]

We would be foolish to limit our view of perceived issues in the world today to mere political polarisation, geopolitical tensions, and the rise of adolescent anxiety. We all know this is far from the whole story.

The same world we live in is often described as 'broken' in the media reporting all around us.

Joaquin Phoenix put it into perspective when he spoke at the 92nd Academy Awards in 2019. What he had to say nearly broke the internet, and for good reason. He received an award for Best Actor for his performance in the film *Joker*. But the speech he delivered was somewhat unexpected. Joaquin's words ring true for many:

Whether we're talking about gender inequality, racism, queer rights or indigenous rights or animal rights, we're talking about the fight against injustice.

2019 was the year for rioting and protests. The world was shocked when rioting over the rise in subway fares began in Santiago, Chile. But the problems in Chile were like boiling water in a pot. It was inevitably going to boil over and cause chaos.

A writer for *Time Magazine*, Rachel Bunyan, reported on the story as it developed in October 2019. Hundreds of thousands of Chilean citizens took to the streets and rioted in a destructive, violent way that ultimately resulted in eighteen individuals losing their lives.[4] In response to the rise in fares, several high school and university students jumped over the barriers to the subways and refused to pay the fine. The young protesters, also experiencing the strain of an underfunded education system, were joined in a mass demonstration by many other Chileans. The participants were equally frustrated with rising living costs, low wages, and one of the worst rates of inequality Latin America had seen.[5]

It wasn't only Chile experiencing riots and unrest. Hong Kong had a similar experience in 2019 when crowds started gathering in the streets. At first, it was slow, and only small groups were gathered, but this grew into a sea of protestors. By late afternoon on 12 June 2019, tens of thousands of protestors had gathered on the streets, outraged by the threat of their freedoms being taken away by a government they inherently saw as a foreign power.

The unrest began to rise. But for those of you that know your history of Hong Kong, the city has a reputation for quashing riots very quickly, silencing the protestors. But not this time. This was different. People on the street at the time observed a different feel to this uprising: the air was filled with a potent mix of 'anxiety, hope, and anger.'[6]

With the crowd growing, global news stations started to report on the brutality at the hands of the Hong Kong police. Accusations later emerged over the misuse of tear gas, pepper spray, and barrages of rubber bullets; all fired into what was, by most accounts, a relatively quiet and peaceful crowd that just wanted to be heard.

The protests were certainly not just about the new extradition law, although that might have been the final straw. Instead, if you looked behind the media coverage, you would notice a deeper motive stemming from straining social tensions that had been bubbling under the surface for years.

If we look twelve months prior, we see the launch of Hong Kong-raised author Xu Xi's book, *Insignificance: Hong Kong Stories*. Her book paints a picture of the rising encroachment of freedoms. Her story covers life in a city where protests were snuffed out quicker than they started. The general population suffered feelings of the Chinese policy of 'One country, two systems', being more a case of 'One country, one system'.

It didn't take long for the proposed extradition law to be suspended, which happened on 15 June. But it didn't mean the people's issues with how things were run were over. The next day, two million people, around twenty-five per cent of the population in Hong Kong, joined a new protest. This time, the focus was unique – it was on the displays of police brutality running rampant across the country.

The world is in flux, and everybody knows it. Perhaps even Miley Cyrus, who exclaimed during an interview with *Elle Magazine*, 'The world is angry!', knows it. Miley wasn't referring to the riots or the political divide seen in the China-US trade war, the US election, or Brexit. And she certainly wasn't talking about the social unrest of Hong Kong, Chile, or the French Gilet Jaune. Instead, Miley was talking about her plans for having a family; her focus was on the environment. For some, she aptly views the world as a 'piece of shit' that's not worth bringing a new life into any time soon.[7]

As Greta Thunberg aptly puts it: 'the ecosystems are collapsing'. And along with it, she claims that her childhood dreams have been stolen.

Let's consider that New York City, a city so powerful and buzzing that it's assumed to be invincible, has fallen victim to climate change. The city has had to launch a vast climate resiliency project to stop the city from becoming submerged. As a result, a whopping 836 km of coastline may suffer from a 20–75 cm rise in sea levels by 2050, putting Manhattan in the most danger and, with time, the rest of New York.[8]

A host of natural disasters hit the earth in 2021, showing just how 'angry' the environment is. Heavy rains battered Brazil and Madagascar, heavy snowfall made its way to Pakistan and Turkey, volcanic eruptions plagued Ecuador, and wildfires spread across Argentina and Spain. What more could we want or need to show us that the world as we know it is changing?[9]

In September 2020, Google showed that 'inequality' was searched more times than in the engine's entire history. But even this lagged far behind more visceral terms like 'revolution' and 'riot.'

The world we know today is far different than it was even a few years ago, and people feel it. Turn on the news today, talk to a friend, or go onto social media, and you're likely to be bombarded with news of another event, tragedy, or issue our planet faces. Race riots, political corruption, a global pandemic, and more recently, threats of war, have seemingly caused the world to become more divided.

For more clarity, let's consider the doomsday clock – a concept created by Albert Einstein in 1945. Initially, it was an idea and way to indicate how close we are to a nuclear Armageddon, with nuclear weapons made just two years before.

The midnight stroke was an illustrative 'game over' moment, encouraging us to think about how close we are to such an event. Today the clock is not just focused on the threat of atomic weapons. However, they're still a vital component of the overall assessment, along with climate change, disruptive technology, and anything else that has the potential to bring with it catastrophic outcomes.

On 20 January 2022, the clock was updated, and while it didn't get any closer, it remained the closest it's ever been to midnight in its history. The metaphorical one hundred seconds from Armageddon looms closer than during the Cold War. Several things were behind this move. The current geopolitical bickering and its potential to turn into a new nuclear arms race were one.[10]

If we take the events of this chapter at face value, then perhaps we have to agree with Miley; maybe this is not a world where one wants to raise children.

But, before we jump to this conclusion, just how accurate are our perceptions?

And importantly, when we're in a state of uncertainty, anxiety, and fear, is everything as bad as it seems?

Chapter 2

Pessimistic Predictions

∞

Ehrlich came out in 1969 to say that he'd take even odds on a bet that by the year 2000, England wouldn't exist.[11]

But sitting here, in the year 2022, just about twenty miles from the English border in my cottage on the North Wales coastline, I can confirm he was wrong. England, despite its political dramas in recent years, remains. At least for now.

The premise of Ehrlich's argument was laid out in his book, *The Population Bomb*, and centred around the simple idea that the rising population was not being fed enough, and innovation would be too slow to catch up. Combine these two things, and you get a situation where starvation abounds.

Ehrlich's solution was to 'rapidly bring the world population under control, reducing the growth rate to zero or making it negative' (Ehrlich, 1968).[12]

Ehrlich of course wasn't the first doomsayer to 'predict' such an apocalyptic event in the world. If we go back a couple of hundred years, we find Malthus, famous for a very similar prediction, and convinced that the growing world population would have to peak.

By Malthus's calculations, the world's population was simply unsustainable – there was not enough food to go around – and this would almost inevitably lead to war, famine, and mass starvation ending only when the population had been reduced sufficiently to match the food output at the time.

In hindsight, we know that the last three centuries weren't one of population decline: it's been a time of rapid population growth. At the same time, food has not run out and has in many cases become more abundant.

Turning to the population data, in 1800, the population was just fifteen per cent of today's. And while we could point to the fact that there have been numerous wars, and unfortunately, there have been times of famine over these years, they do not come from the same causes that Malthus was pointing to. Innovation did keep up – and more.

What Malthus and Ehrlich missed was the level and pace of innovation that would occur. That infrastructure, production systems, and methods would increase crop yields massively.[13] Medical advances would allow us to combat disease. Our understanding of nutrition would leap forward. They didn't understand that the speed of innovation is not constant: at times, it jumps.

This is not to say that just because two doomsayers got it wrong in the past, we simply kick back and ignore these issues around us today. Greta and Miley have valid points that we should pay attention to. After all, there are some pretty big things that we need to put right in the world.

But then, both Malthus and Ehrlich had valid points too.

My point is it's easy to get trapped in Malthus's way of thinking. To see only insurmountable obstacles and hurdles, not the future innovation that is always bubbling under the surface.

The human race's history is one of overcoming impossible odds. Time and time again, we have found ourselves in situations that we simply should not have walked away from.

This is not some freak accident or luck. But rather at its heart, is the most remarkable ability of the human race. Our ability to adapt, create and innovate.

Population growth and technological advances

Malthus was born ten years before the Industrial Revolution started to take hold in Britain. The central thesis of Malthus' argument was that the population was simply too big and theorised it would grow exponentially. In contrast, the supply and availability of food would only grow at a far slower, linear pace.

Combining these two thoughts lets us see where Malthus was coming from.

Just as Malthus predicted, the UK's population grew rapidly, climbing from 5.5 million in 1700 to over 9 million by 1800.[14] Malthus was himself part of this 'baby boom', born in 1766. But the UK's population didn't stop there. It kept growing, reaching 17.9 million by 1851 – just seventeen years after Malthus' death.

Today these numbers seem paltry; the population has nearly quadrupled since to stand at an estimated 67.4 million in 2022.

The part that Malthus got wrong was the increase in food supply. He vastly underestimated the power of innovation, believing to his detriment that innovation would, and could, only increase at a slow pace.

This assumption was not as misplaced as it may at first seem. Like most of us, he witnessed far more incremental innovation than radical innovation.

So, before we ridicule Malthus for being so short-sighted, we first need to acknowledge just how easy it is for us to get caught in this same trap. Our brains are anticipatory devices.[15] Suppose we see innovation and technological development as something that ticks along in the background, and see innovation as a constant, incremental process. In that case, we too start to formulate a dim view of the future.

Take the current pace of change occurring in the energy sector. The move away from hydrocarbons is, at this point, nowhere near sufficient to meet the target set at the 2015 Paris Climate Accords.

But change does not always occur in a smooth, incremental fashion. Breakthroughs occur that radically change the way things are done – and the pace of progress.

A Time of Change

The eighteenth century in Britain, and Europe in general, ushered in massive improvements in farming and agriculture, adopting new techniques and replacing old inefficient ones.

Farmers started to implement ideas that may seem basic today but were revolutionary then.

These ideas changed how the lands were managed, introducing better crop rotations that would increase crop yields and bring a far greater variety of foods. What became known as the four-field rotation system, first implemented by farmers in parts of France, allowed the soils to regain nutrient content and fertility far better than previous methods and understanding.

The increase in crop yields not only fed the people but also allowed farmers to increase the level of livestock through increased feed supply at a reduced cost.

While these changes improved the efficiency of farming and overcame the issues that Malthus had foreseen, it's not to say that all aspects of this change were initially positive.

Something that we'll see time and time again throughout this book is that these points of transition aren't typically smooth for society. In fact, by their nature, they are highly disruptive and force society on a path of reorganisation around the new production systems of the day.

Living in highly complex societies, a change in one area can, and often does, cause broad sweeping changes in nearly all aspects of life.The metaphor that a butterfly flaps its wings in the Amazonian jungle and subsequently a storm ravages half of Europe is true when we're talking about change and innovation in the world.

The increasing efficiency of farming and agriculture, and the growing population, also brought about a change in the physical landscape. While there had been a drive towards more enclosed farmland since the twelfth century in Britain, there was a renewed motivation behind this.

The Enclosed Act of 1773 was a fundamental force in the change of use in much land that was previously 'common land'. Open spaces that several people called 'commoners' collectively had rights over and could use for grazing their animals, collecting firewood, and cutting turf for burning.

The new farming techniques required segregated fields, marked-off and fenced. While these commons were much enjoyed and used, they were not owned by the commoners. The commoners simply had rights over them.

With increasing profits from modern farming on the horizon, there were new incentives from landowners and tenant farmers to re-purpose the common lands. Both parties saw this as a way to increase incomes. For the tenant farmers, there was an expectation that the efficiency of land would increase and, in turn, the output from their efforts. For the landowners, it was a chance to rewrite the tenancy agreements and increase the rent based on the new output expectations.[16] The Enclosed Act made this possible.

As the common land started to disappear, small holders who had used the land to help support their way of life found themselves without land to rear animals, nor access to forests to gather firewood.

In total, by 1914, some twenty per cent of the land of England, 6.8 million acres, had been enclosed.[17]

It is perhaps no surprise that the Enclosed Act was met with enormous public resistance. It directly affected those who had built their lives on the idea that access to these lands would be a constant, unwavering right.

The net migration from the countryside to urban areas shouldn't be underestimated. In fact, many historians cite it as one of the most important features of nineteenth century Britain, with up to forty per cent of the growth in urban populations being attributed to this.[18]

Of course, it would be an oversimplification to think or suggest that the internal migration of Britain at this time was solely down to a change in land usage. Of course, we know it was not. The lure of higher wages in the industrialised cities also drew people in.

It wasn't just internal migration leading to growth in urban locations. Immigration played an important role too, with the Irish making up one of the largest groups, again lured by the newly industrialised world on show. Later, this immigration rate picked up pace from Ireland with the potato famine taking hold in the 1840s.

Today we stand at a very similar point

Today we stand at a very similar point to Malthus and Ehrlich. The future, by many measures, looks daunting and bleak.

While Malthus' concerns were centred on food, ours are centred on emissions, global temperatures, fears of collapsing ecosystems, and inequality.

Let's take climate change: if the temperature of the world increases by more than two degrees Celsius, then we are warned that there could be catastrophic consequences for humanity and the world's ecosystems. Water shortages alone could affect some three billion people.[19]

To prevent this, we must cut, by 2030, the emission of greenhouse gases by ninety per cent.[20] To put the magnitude of this in perspective, with all its lockdowns and reduction in travel 2020 only saw greenhouse gasses cut by a mere 6.4 per cent.[21]

Just as in Malthus's day, the issues we see around us are very real, looming large over us. But we'd do well to remember that the human capacity to overcome the odds and innovate our way through issues is equally impressive – if not more so. If there is one 'norm' that we can attribute to the journey of the human race it is this: we are exceptional at overcoming the seemingly impossible.

In 2015 the Member states of the United Nations came together and devised a blueprint for what they called 'peace and prosperity'. In other words, they drew up a list of seventeen areas of life that we need to work and improve on to ensure that the planet remains a place where human activity and life can thrive, both now and in the future.

With the direction of development goals now set, innovation is already being unleashed at break-neck pace. Take, for example, the birth of vertical farms that can reduce water usage compared to traditional farming. Or the progress made in the ability of solar panels to capture the sun's rays. Or even the more general push for cleaner, kinder companies around the world. Change is already happening if we look closely.

Taking a step back

It was the summer of 2021, and I'd reached out to Prof Martin Chick, Professor of economic history at Edinburgh University, after reading the highlights from a talk he'd given just a few days before at a conference I'd unfortunately missed.

My intention was to see if he'd be willing to jump on a podcast and record a conversation about the importance of history when looking to the future. It's a precarious topic to suggest to a historian. Why? Well, the purists like Steve Manson, professor of history at the University of Groningen in the Netherlands, believe that history should come with a health warning for those who want to learn lessons from it.

I get it. I get Manson's perspective. And in some ways, he's right, too. Each historical event is unique, with complex drivers, tailwinds, and headwinds. There is no way that you can – or perhaps should – extrapolate this to the future. You should certainly not expect history to repeat itself like some cyclical conveyor belt that spits out the same events repeatedly.

But that's not to say that history can't teach us valuable lessons. There are patterns to things that occur that we should pay close attention to. This is very different from using these patterns and signals to try and predict as Malthus and Ehrlich did. That is foolhardy and not recommended. But prediction is a long shot away from awareness and insight.

Take the economists for example. While many good economists out there do great work, the issue the profession has faced in recent decades is that their models fail to reflect the real world they're supposed to represent.

While their models use elegant and often sophisticated maths, they have a flaw. They underestimate the small, infrequent, yet highly influential events. And these supposedly rare events, well, let's just say they have a habit of showing up far more than you'd think.

In other words, their models, like Malthus, assume that almost all things only make slight deviations from their path. They have failed to take into account the lesson of history: that progress and change are not always smooth and sometimes jump.

History, as a field of enquiry, has made its changes in the modern era, too, adopting a far more scientific approach. An outcome of this is that historical research today is far more focused on ever shorter periods of time.

According to the author of *The End Is Always Near*, Dan Carlin, this change started in the mid-twentieth century. Prior to this modern school of thought, which posits that 'history teaches you nothing', historical research found merit in looking back and at least discerning moral lessons from the past – seeing its patterns and transitions. So, while I agree with Mason that expecting events to replay themselves exactly is a fool's errand, there is merit in observing the patterns and cycles of change.

This is something I fully encourage us to re-incorporate if we are to see the changes going on around us.

Martin agreed to talk, but he made it clear he held reservations about jumping on the podcast.

I took the positives and ignored the reservations – hoping I'd be able to overcome them if given a chance to show my passion for the topic. *That's great.* I went back to him on LinkedIn InMail. I followed up with, *I'm not going to try and twist your arm about the podcast if you don't feel this is a good fit for you. But I firmly believe that looking backwards has a big place in looking forwards. Too many people are oblivious to the past.*

The meeting was set. I didn't really know what to expect. One thing I knew for sure, with his reservations about the podcast, I needed a question to break the ice.

I went in with a safe opener. *Martin, so what are you working on right now?*

The answer given by this jolly mild-mannered professor I met on Zoom blew my mind. I'll have to paraphrase, but his response went something like, '*Oh, I'm just working on a new book, and currently researching how the laws that govern the deep seabed were arrived at. I think when we get to space these might well be the blueprint that is used.*'

I'll be honest, while I think a lot about the future in my job and the writing of this book, I'd never even considered the legal structure of space.

Our ten-minute chat turned into an hour, and while it ended with Martin still unsure about a podcast, there was a fundamental point we'd both agreed on. The idea of the Fourth Industrial Revolution, a concept pushed by Klaus Schwab, Executive Chairman of the World Economic Forum, is an understatement.

The changes we're likely to see coming in the next few years or decades are less akin to the First Industrial Revolution, or even the recent information technology age we have just been through. Instead, the change that is coming is far more momentous than this. It is far more likely to be on a magnitude we saw in the transition from being roaming hunter-gatherers to settled agrarian societies some ten thousand years ago.

What we have discussed so far is essential for two main reasons. First, we shouldn't fall into the trap of expecting progress to always be linear, constant, or even smooth. And secondly, transitions, at least in the shorter term, are highly disruptive and bring uncertain times.

The cycles of change

The innovation cycle is the main focus of this book. This fairly regular pattern of paradigm-shifting technology changes the structure of business, regulation, production, and even society.

But there are more changes afoot today than just the innovation cycle. In fact, there are at least three other cycles that we should be aware of that are also on the move. These include shifting global superpowers, the third information revolution, and the step-change in the production cycle.

The advent of AI and machine learning has also sped up innovation. More likely than not, when the next wave of technology comes, the paradigm it brings is likely to be unleashed faster than we've seen with previous cycles.

Additional acceleration may also come from policy surrounding climate change.

But it is not only the pace of change this time that we need to think about.

Behind these changes are a number of highly potent forces. For one, there are signs that America's exceptionalism as the world's hyperpower is fading. This is not to say the shifting of global power will be a quick one, but instead we should be aware that transitions of this magnitude are often accompanied by periods of increased social and political tensions. The previous transition was between the UK and the US, which saw the devastating events of World War I and II.

To find the one previous to this, we must turn back before the Industrial Revolution to the Anglo-Dutch Wars and the long-drawn-out period of naval conflict.

The point is that global superpowers don't transition all that often, but their effects can be felt far and wide when they do.

Today, America's reign as a hyperpower is already fading. It is too early to say how long this will take, or even if China will manage to step up, but the early signs are there to be watched.

The other change we should take note of is the third information revolution. We will look at this in far more detail later, as it's perhaps one of the most powerful transformational forces we know. The first information revolution occurred in the fifteenth century, followed by the second in the nineteenth century.

On both occasions, the increased level of shared information significantly changed society's understanding and core philosophy.

Today, the full deployment of technologies that blur the lines between virtual and physical worlds are the next iteration we will live through.

If these factors are not enough to paint the picture of why this transition is likely to be more significant, and of a greater magnitude, then we must also consider the change in the *production principle*.

To appreciate this, we need to take an even larger step back. Not looking at human change over decades or centuries, but rather millennia. Over this time frame of world history and human development, we see four distinct phases or *production principles*. Generally, this can be broken down into the hunter-gather phase, followed by the craft-agrarian phase. As we enter the fifteenth century, we arrive at the more familiar trade-industrial phase.

But the trade-industrial phase started to end in the 1970s, with the development of the information technology era.

The phase we've just entered shares common characteristics with the trade-industrial phase, but it also stands apart. It forms what appears to be the beginning of an entirely new production paradigm that we call the scientific-cybernetic phase.[22]

This phase will usher in a time that sees to the blurring of virtual and physical worlds and information systems that are self-regulating, self-learning, and even organic.

Changes in the production principle are very infrequent events. Such change has occurred only three times in the past ten thousand years, and only four times in human history.

The culmination of all these events at once makes seeing and understanding the changes all the more critical.

We must learn how we can get better at seeing them and understanding how our individual perspectives can affect this ability.

As Ted Casby put it in *Closing the Mind Gap,* 'when our beliefs are poorly calibrated to the world, our responses are ineffective and our power is undermined' (Cadsby, 2014).

That is the task that we are faced with today: to remain calibrated with the world so our responses remain effective and appropriate. We must also ensure that change does not overwhelm or burn us out.

My children inspired the motivation for initially writing this book. But as the material was pulled together, and from the countless conversations I had with people worldwide, there seemed to be an appeal from a much wider audience.

I am far from having all the answers, and I don't profess to have a crystal ball. However, I hope this framework delivers a deeper understanding of change and how we think, allowing you to see the world with more clarity and less uncertainty. From this, I hope you will gain a deep-rooted confidence and optimism in the innovative and creative abilities of the human condition.

Before we end this chapter, let's return to the point made at the start. Are we making the same mistakes as Malthus and Ehrlich with our pessimistic predictions?

Are our perceptions skewed toward the negative? Or have Miley and Greta got it right?

Bob Duffy, Director of The Policy Institute at King's College London, and former Chairman of Ipsos MORI Social Research Institute, was for a long time involved in the Ipsos global Perils of Perception survey. A survey that covered more than forty countries and focused on answering the question of just how accurately we see the world.

The title of his book *Perils of Perception: why we're wrong about nearly everything* probably gives away his research findings.

In their 2017 study, titled: *Perceptions are not reality: things are NOT as bad as they seem*, they demonstrated that most people were way off when asked simple questions about murder rates, terrorism, and teenage pregnancy – viewing the world as a far dimmer, darker place than it is in reality.[23]

This idea is frequently backed up when researchers ask questions about the state of the world. Their inquiries may include factors such as the risk of overpopulation, the progress of child mortality, literacy rates, vaccination status, the rate of female education, employment, and voting rights – all areas that have gone through rapid progress in a relatively short period of time. While there is more to be done in these areas, the trend is clear. It's incredibly positive and continuing.

Before we dive into understanding the innovation cycle, let's first consider just how far we've come. It's a meaningful way to frame the discussions we're going to have, and an inspiring journey that points not only to where we've come from but also to where we're heading.

Chapter 3

Just How Far We've Come

∞

It was 15 December, and a prosperous baker in a European city was making his final preparations for the festive period. He'd spent the day browsing, visiting numerous shops, and buying gifts for his family and friends.

Meanwhile, his wife had been busy decorating the house, ready and excited to show off the new marble she'd installed in the home just a few months ago. The marble had been specially sourced and shipped from Greece, and to be fair, it was a stunning focal piece.

Back in the city, the baker was fighting his way through the bustling high street, quietly pleased with the purchases he'd made. He could already picture his family's faces when they received them – perfume from the Middle East for his wife, and the latest toys for his younger children.

For this eldest boy, a collection of the best books that money could buy – in the original Greek, too. Plato and Aristotle didn't mean much to the baker, who was bourgeois through and through, but he valued education and where that could take a person; a chance at a government position perhaps. The opportunities are endless.

But unknown to the baker, his world was about to change forever.

In just a few short weeks, the system of peace he'd known his entire life, even before his grandparents were born, was about to end.[24]

It was the Saturnalia of 192 AD, the mid-December ancient Roman festival honouring the agriculture god, Saturn. But this would be the last Saturnalia of the Pax Romana era, a two-hundred-year period often heralded as the 'golden age' given its unusually long period of peace and prosperity.

The times that followed would see an organised, systemic oppression by kings and popes. Placing faith over reason and making logic and progress the enemies of the state; ultimately dooming millions of people to die in servitude, ignorance, and poverty.

Fast forward to the present day, and the life of this Roman baker seems almost primitive to any of us living in the developed world. While our baker had the appearance of modern-day luxury, what he lacked was far greater. He lacked what we would call basic necessities.[25]

Take poliovirus. Today there remains no cure. In severe cases, the virus can infect the person's spinal cord leading to paralysis, and at its worst, victims die when they can no longer breathe. This is just one of many diseases that we now routinely vaccinate for. He, nor his children, had access to the vaccines we take for granted today.

If our baker or his family became ill, his doctor would have prescribed him the 'latest' remedy of the day (likely various animal entrails mixed at the full moon).[26]

Whatever measure we use, there is very little part of his life that we would willingly trade for our own.

What's more, we gradually move exponentially from his point of prosperity to even greater heights that would simply be unimaginable to our baker.

This comparison of the modern day to the past can be easily summed up in two words: interconnectivity and innovation. Between these two ideas lies all our progress. Run through a standard day in the baker's life and compare it to our own and it is likely to bring with it the eye-widening realisation of just how incomparable and incredible we have it today.

The Simple Luxury of Sleep

In 2018, Garmin upgraded the sleep-tracking capabilities of their smartwatches – changing from a simple measurement of movement and heart rate to what they call Advanced Sleep Monitoring or ASM. In addition to heart rate and motion, many of the new Garmin range also bring in data from oxygen levels and respiration rates. Of course, Garmin wasn't the only one pushing new technology in this area with the sleep business booming over the last few years.

While these devices don't measure sleep directly, they bring awareness of sleep patterns and the correlations between the quality of our sleep and factors such as exercise or alcohol intake before bed. In the words of Dr. Alan Schwartz, director of the Sleep Disorder Centre at John Hopkins Bayview Medical Centre they '*give you something to reflect on*'.[27]

The rise of sleep tracking is not that unsurprising; in today's modern world sleep issues are on the rise. We're stressed, and most sleep experts conclude that this comes from things such as a sedentary lifestyle, and the rise of stress and concerns about work, our health, and finances.

But before we jump on the bandwagon of just how bad this modern world is for us, most of us still have a regular opportunity to get our heads down for a solid seven to eight hours of undisturbed sleep – and in a bed. That's something to celebrate.[28]

This 'luxury' is a surprisingly modern one. Until the Industrial Revolution, people most commonly slept in four-hour blocks; starting when they came home, too physically exhausted from the day's manual labour for anything else. So, they went to bed and slept until night.

After a few hours of sleep, rested enough to gain a little energy, they'd commence the labour-intensive routines of cooking and housework before returning to their second sleep a few hours later.[29]

It wasn't just physical work that took away from the quality of our sleep. There is the consideration of security, too.

Once we close our doors at night, many of us rest easy on the assumption that we're relatively safe. There is, for most people, a low chance that somebody will simply walk into our house without an invitation. And very few of us will ever have to encounter an intruder.

However, this concept that no one can enter your home without permission would be a dream in past eras, including for our Roman baker. And it wasn't just thieves, murderers, and bandits you had to worry about. A state official may walk in at any time, too.

From the medieval serf to the Egyptian labourer – your life was a function of the state and at the mercy of its ruler.[30] You were not an objective part of the economy, but rather a subjective one.

If it was decreed that you should move, join the army, or just be taken out for any number of reasons, all a monarch or dictator had to do was click their fingers and you were as good as gone.

This was also not a class issue. During the reigns of both Nero and Tiberius, everyone from fisherman to senators were at the mercy of their ruler and could be removed at any moment.

Today, human rights provide us with some protection, but we should remember that these have only been safeguarded in a few countries for over a century. And we've seen significant increases in their scope only in the last seventy years.[32]

Take Europe up to the 1930s. If you were anywhere east of the Rhine, then being *disappeared* would have been part of government policy.

Returning to just how good we have it today, if we stray just a little way from the basic necessity of sleep, we find yet more revolutionary phenomena in our modern times.

What we would consider simple things today were labour-intensive and time-consuming tasks to those living a few hundred years ago.

From kitchens with electric hobs replacing dirty coal fires, to lights that we can turn on with the flick of a switch – or even our voice. Even the idea of 'going to the bathroom' is a concept utterly foreign to past generations.

To reach the dizzying heights of the modern bathroom, you first require a room where water can freely flow in and out – and without modern plumbing, that isn't easy. Add to this the need for inlets and outlets, and the need for a drainage system that carries away the waste.

For centuries, this kind of technology simply didn't exist. Therefore, toilets remained little more than a hole in the ground while sinks were just a cold jug of water.

Since these dramatic technological improvements, the act of washing has gone from a difficult endeavour to an enjoyable daily activity. One would think nothing of jumping in the shower with hot water gushing down. In fact, as we'll look at in a later chapter, we find modern bathing so relaxing and calming many do it just to get some headspace.

Compare this to how our ancestors had to go about this task. If you were in the depths of winter (remembering that Europe went through a mini ice age from 1300–1850)[33] and fancied a wash, it could be the last trip you ever made. Water had to be drawn from wells, and it was quite common for people to fall in while doing so, with drownings being cited as the highest cause of accidental deaths in London during medieval times.[34]

Alongside our increasing technological capabilities, our understanding of the importance of simple daily rituals such as washing has increased. Hand washing was a staple ritual for many medieval people, but the practice had fallen away by the eighteenth century, showing that it was done more out of tradition than knowledge of germ theory.[35] Miasma theory, the dominant view in the western world at the time, suggested that diseases were caused by bad smells, rather than germs. Washing hands under this concept was nowhere near as important as not inhaling the air around a sick person.[36]

Today such thinking seems ludicrously primitive. And with our modern understanding, perhaps it is. But when we come to consider the world around us, we'd do well to consider just where we have come from, and the significant leaps forward we have made, because future generations will likely look back at our time similarly.

One such leap forward is our increasing ability to travel and navigate the globe. Traveling from the UK to the US today takes just a few hours. Hop on an early morning plane in London and you could be sat in New York for tea. Even at the peak of Victorian travel, it still took five days.[37] One hundred years before that, in the 1700s, it was twenty-one days, and in the 1600s, it was five weeks. Go much further back and the voyage was unheard of outside of St Brendan and Eric the Red, whose voyages may be mere legend.

But this increased ability to travel is not just about having luxury holidays; it is the role faster transport plays in the foods that we eat, the variety we have on offer to us, and even the cost of such items. This is something that we pay little attention to. Yet we should be staggeringly grateful for all our technological advancements, not to mention the countless expeditions and lives that were lost to bring this about.

To put this in perspective, even those today with mediocre incomes, if they also have a modern-day supermarket in their town, they likely have more food choices and varieties at their fingertips than even the richest of rulers and kings could have dreamt of having at their infamous banquets in eras gone by.

But in most conversations about the state of the world today, we skip over the incredible stories about the increases in quality of life that have been seen. Today, pessimism reigns. If you believe that we live in a golden age, or there has never been a better time to be alive, then you are in a tiny minority.

Studies keep showing that it is not just general improvements in the quality of our life. From access to running water, better sanitation, and food choices, decreases in infant mortality, increase in life expectancy and medical care have all been areas of unbelievable improvements over the past one hundred years.

During this period, poverty has been meaningfully reduced too. Go back to the 1800s in Britain and it was not just inequality but widespread poverty, too. Malnutrition was rife, with twenty-five per cent of child mortality occurring because they simply did not have enough food.

Today, we have the opposite problem. Food is so abundant and our diets so rich that our risk is less about starvation and more about the health consequences of consuming such highly calorific diets, particularly when technology has, for most, reduced the need for physical exertion.

Our understanding of the world from a scientific perspective is also growing – exponentially in some areas. Companies at the heart of the manufacturing world have used this to significantly change how they make products. The increase in use of recycled material over virgin materials is just one such example.

We are also learning quickly to choose products with less environmental impact and use fewer resources in the process.

In the modern free-market age, we as consumers have abundant choices and are ultimately endowed with choosing which companies and production methods we favour.

Andrew McAfee, the author of the book *More from Less,* showcases that these changes are not things we hope to happen in the future – they are already happening around us and have been for some time.

The idea that prosperity only occurs at the expense of the natural environment is a theory connected to a past age. It applied to the early Industrial Revolution. But as we became aware of the impact of greenhouse gasses through the work of scientists such as Svante Arrhenius,[ii] we have been changing the way we do things ever since – making energy-intensive processes more efficient and developing better ways to produce items with less impact.

In other words, we stand at a point in time, for the very first time, where we are starting to harness all our scientific and technological understanding to maintain general prosperity while also having far less impact on the environment to produce the goods we use every day.

Of course, there is more work to be done. But when things become important to us as humans, history is pretty clear: our creativity and innovation rise to become undeniably impressive.

Alas, those pushing overly negative outlooks capture the limelight. Negative titles and stories grab and hold our attention far more than the positive story of steady progress.

The amount of news we consume affects our perceptions too. A few years ago, our news consumption was limited to the printed morning paper and the regular news slots on radio and TV. That was it. The issue with this, as we will look at later, is the more you hear something, the more inclined you'll be to believe it occurs frequently, which is not always the case.

This is not to say there is nothing wrong in the world. There are many areas of legitimate concern with the natural environment. There also are areas of the natural environment that have gone through incredible stories of positive transformation over the past few decades.

In 2011, the annual report from British Waterways marked fifty years of targeted and concentrated efforts to improve the conditions of the rivers, canals, and reservoirs around the British Isles. Many were in a pretty bad way. Let's take the River Thames that runs through the heart of London. Declared biologically dead since 1857, it is now the location of marine life and even annual fishing competitions.

It wasn't just the Thames. The report from the British Waterways noted, 'the underlying condition of our waterways has not been so good in many years'.[38]

The point is, real progress is made when we start to take active steps towards bringing about positive change, such as cutting the level of environmental impact in production processes or commencing conservation projects.

Zooming all the way out from the improvements of waterways, since the early 1980s, NASA and NOAA (National Oceanic and Atmospheric Administration) satellites have been whizzing around above our heads at about 17,000 mph, taking photos. Thousands of them, in fact.

This data has been a goldmine for researchers such as Prof. Ranga Myneni and his Ph.D. students working out of Boston University in the USA, as well as Dr. Jarle W. Bjerke and Dr. Hans Tommervik at the Norwegian Institute for Nature Research.

But what caught their eye?

Well, for one, the world is getting greener.

In a paper published in the *Journal of Nature Reviews Earth and Environment,* the Norwegians Dr Bejerke and Dr Tommervik reveal that all this increase in CO_2 is having a noticeable effect on plant life: it's growing faster and helping slow the rate of warming.

Green plants grow faster in the presence of higher CO_2 levels. On top of this, their water usage becomes far more efficient, making them more drought resistant. It's been the main driver behind the re-greening of the Earth's surface in the past forty years.

But what was most telling from the Norwegian researchers' paper was the cooling effect this has already had on temperatures. The temperature effects of global warming would have been around twenty-five per cent greater if not for the increase in vegetation.

We have a lot of work to do on global issues. Still, if there is one core message this chapter tries to deliver, it's this. When we put our minds to it, humans are incredible at getting the seemingly impossible done. There is also an awful lot that we perceive as being far worse than it actually is.

Hans Rosling, co-founder of the Gapminder Foundation, describes his life mission to rid the world of what he labels global ignorance.

In his book, *Factfulness: Ten Reasons We're Wrong About the World – and Why Things Are Better Than You Think*, Hans encourages us to think about child mortality as a proxy for progress – with good reason. Babies are fragile and therefore need safe, clean environments, typically with access to well-educated nurses and doctors to survive. In other words, a low child mortality rate signifies a lot of technological innovation and understanding.

If we take this measure, child mortality rates have been cut dramatically in the past few decades, not exclusively in developed countries but as part of a global phenomenon. The global average has declined from over forty percent in the 1800s, to just 4.5 per cent today.[39]

If we bring this back to the Roman baker we met at the start of this chapter, when we step back from all the apparent sophistication of his time, this simple fact alone points to a very different life experience. The children he had were in all likelihood not the full story of the ones that had been born.

So back to Miley and Greta's view. Is this really such a piece-of-shit world? And has the modern era stolen the childhoods of millions? I will let you decide the answers to those.

To understand why our views are so dim of the world around us, we need to better understand our brains on uncertainty, which is precisely where we'll go next.

Chapter 4

Our Brains on Uncertainty

∞

Before we go any further, let's get one thing straight. Your brain hates uncertainty.

It can't stand it.

It hates ambiguity.

It hates not knowing, to the point it craves certainty and clarity even if those things aren't available.

While it's true that some people are naturally better at coping with uncertainty, and yes, we can train ourselves to cope a little better with it, we're naturally wired to avoid it at all costs.

It's a process that has been refined over thousands of years, and with good reason. Eons ago when we lived in dark dank caves, the unfamiliar, unknown situation was a fairly reliable sign of imminent danger. These feelings made us sit up, take note, and sometimes run in the opposite direction.

In the distant past, change was something to fear. On the other hand, a familiar routine and doing things the way we'd always done them was 'safe', and our brains duly rewarded us for this with the feeling of comfort.

Bring this forward to our present day and our world is different, but our response is not.

Change today is part of life, not something to run from. Yet, we still cling to the status quo, the familiar – the old, safe ways.

But ask yourself this, do old ways remain safe, or even relevant, in the future? Isn't it the status quo that is the very thing that's about to be ripped up and re-written?

There is a glaringly obvious issue; the rules of the old cave dwelling world have flipped. The world changed and nobody told you. I would argue that since the information technology age commencing in the 1970s, standing still and clinging to the *'old ways'* is now the biggest threat to the quality of our lives. Being open to new ideas and new ways of doing is the way to progress. But our brains have not yet caught up. We have what Ted Cadsby calls the brain-world gap, and as change speeds up in the world, that gap is growing.

Covid-19

In early 2020, as the Covid-19 pandemic took hold, society saw its day-to-day life change overnight. On a globally unprecedented scale, too. Businesses were shuttered, and all but essential trips away from home were forbidden. In addition to this dramatic change in the way we were living, there was also a whole raft of economic uncertainties for business owners, employees, and policy makers – and to add to this, the uncertainty of illness.

Just how transmissible, and deadly, was this new strain of coronavirus? What was the prognosis for friends and family that caught it? Particularly older relatives? In fact, would we even see them again? And just when would 'normal' life resume?

In psychology, uncertainty can be thought of as simply being the state of 'not knowing'. But we can be more specific about this and think of it in two separate ways: risk and ambiguity.

While both give rise to uncertainty, they're very different. In the case of risk, we might not know the outcome of some event for sure, but we can map out the most likely scenarios. Perhaps even assign some probabilities to them. This could be the kind of uncertainty we face when awaiting exam results, or the results of a medical test.

When we're talking about the future and how it could play out, that's a far more complex system with unknown outcomes to which we simply can't accurately attach probabilities. In this world, uncertainty is not risk, but ambiguity.

Take some of the changes occurring today. What does the advent of artificial intelligence, machine learning, and augmented reality really mean for the future of society? For work? For you?

In the future, will robots take all our jobs or just some? Will new 'human' jobs even spring up? What if robots gain a level of intelligence far beyond our own and become our overlords?

What happens to identities, gender, age, and race when we fully integrate into a world that blends the virtual and physical? Is it positive or negative for society? Does it add to inequity or eradicate it?

Ambiguity is very different from risk. It comes with far deeper unknowns.

At key points of change, like today, there is a lot of ambiguity; there is a lot of uncertainty. Our brains struggle to make sense of all that's going on, never mind how it might play out and what direction the world might take next.

At the same time, we can easily become disorientated if we try to stand still at these moments. Our blueprint, or our internal map of how the world works, can quickly become outdated and no longer reflect the world's reality. If this happens, we become disoriented and confused. We don't understand the world – or how it works. We don't know why the results of our actions no longer work when they did just a few years before.

For many people, high exposure to uncertainty typically shows as anxiety, ranging from mild concern to outright panic. Often close behind these feelings, we also find frustration and rage, people becoming increasingly despondent, and maybe even helpless. As the void between what they know and the reality of the current world widens, uncertainty and stress rise.

Our understanding of stress has vastly improved in recent years, and along with it, the link between stress and uncertainty, thanks to ongoing research in the field of neurology. In fact, some researchers suggest it's not so much a link between these two concepts, but rather, they are almost the same[40] – uncertainty and stress are, after all, a lack of control and not having answers to questions.

It is also from the field of neurology that we get a glimpse of why stress can be so tiring and draining. It's something all of us have personal experience with. When we feel uncertain about a situation, be it right now, or one we anticipate in the future, our brains become hypervigilant. They increase the speed at which we gather information, desperately trying to find something that might help dissipate this feeling of uncertainty and lack of control and remove us from the uncomfortable state of unknowing.

Gathering and processing more and more information is an exhausting process. Your brain is an energy-hungry organ at the best of times.

War of the worlds

In late 1938, Orson Welles assembled his team of actors and musicians, a group of exemplary professionals. They'd rehearsed for weeks, perfecting their lines and getting the sound effects right.

As the date swung around, Sunday 30 October 1938, the hard work and hours of practice were done, and it was time to go on air and let the show begin.

It was a prime-time slot that CBS radio had given them, and Orson knew millions of Americans would be tuning in. As a 23-year-old, he certainly didn't let the pressure of this occasion get to him. But there was one thing that he'd overlooked.

On the rival radio channel NBC was the uber-popular prime-time radio show run by ventriloquist Edgar Bergen. While ventriloquism might not be the most naturally suited concept for radio, with the audience having no idea if the ventriloquist's lips were moving or not, the storyline, characters, and interactions of Edgar Bergen made it a hit. It had a loyal following on Sundays at 8 p.m.

Millions would tune in, and this particular night was no exception. Not to worry, the listeners thought, we'll listen to Edgar's *Charlie McCarthy Show* first and then re-tune over to CBS and catch Orson's show. After all, we'll only miss the first few minutes.

As Edgar finished up his performance around 8:12 p.m., millions of listeners did indeed re-tune their radios over to CBS. Orson and the Mercury Theatre were now in full swing. And they were nailing the performance.

The late audience had only missed the first few minutes of the show. But these would prove to be pretty significant on this occasion. They'd missed the broadcaster at the start of the show introducing 'Orson Welles and the Mercury Theatre on the air in War of the Worlds'. This was a seat-gripping performance for those listening right from the start, an adapted version of H.G. Wells' *War of the Worlds* book, first published in 1898.

But those arriving twelve minutes late were tuning in to what could only be described as the end of the world. Someone even claimed to be a reporter on the ground, broadcasting directly from the farmer's field in New Jersey where the asteroid had landed, and the aliens were pouring out.

'something's wriggling out of the shadow like a grey snake. Now there's another one and another one. They look like tentacles to me.' The reporter said, before upping the ante. *'I can hardly force myself to keep looking at it, it's so awful. The eyes are black and gleam like a serpent. The mouth is kind of V-shaped with saliva dripping from its rimless lip that seems to quiver and pulsate.'*[41]

For those of you that know the story of *War of the Worlds*, it only gets worse from there. The Martians were not just terrifying to look at; they were also fully intent on killing any feeble, pathetic humans that got in their path – and did so with relative ease given their heat-ray guns and the poisonous gas that they're not shy to unload.

The performance was convincing. The actors sounded genuinely scared. Uncertainty abounded in the audience's minds, raising stress, anxiety, and genuine fear.

Phone calls to the police, newspaper offices, and radio stations from listeners were sufficient evidence that hysteria had broken out. As well as this and a stampede, Orson received a number of death threats for the heightened emotions he'd given rise to in the audience.

Information seeking

It would be easy to poke fun at this story. Focus on the aspect of it; just how could the people of the 1930s be so easily duped? I mean, come on.

But in mocking what appears to be a naive and primitive time, we miss the point. Our ability to verify facts has increased a million percent since the 1930s. A quick scan of Twitter, Insta, or Google would have not only revealed that no aliens were invading but probably also brought us a host of fun facts about the performers.

We must admit this: it's natural to get caught up in the hype and hysteria of the moment. We do it today, and future generations will likely do it too.

Whether uncertainty is invoked through stories of laser-wielding aliens landing in New Jersey or a crisis hits – be it war, a pandemic, a natural disaster, or financial crisis – there is typically a marked increase in the level of uncertainty, disorientation, and fear where the uncertainty threatens our current way of life.

As the Covid-19 pandemic hit, people's worlds were turned upside down and news and information about the virus spread almost as fast as the virus itself.

Researchers interested in information-seeking behaviours started to look at the public's reaction.

What they found was that people almost immediately started to search for information. Uncertainty rose, and so did the hypervigilance and information-seeking behaviours of the brain. Google search trends reveal that top searches in the first few weeks of Covid reaching Europe included terms such as 'symptoms', 'Wuhan', 'shortness of breath', and 'chest pain', along with attempts to find out what the daily numbers were, and how fast was it spreading.

What is interesting about this is *when* this behaviour started. People didn't wait for local cases to climb, or even for local restrictions to be put in place. Uncertainty about the future was building well before these visible measures came into force. This is a crucial insight into how our vision of the future affects us in the now.

Bento and five other researchers at Indiana University concluded that the first announcements in the media were the trigger.[42] From what they could see, government information was also helping focus people's attention on how best to prepare and cope with the new situation they found themselves in.

Information seeking is our natural response. But this, too, is an area where the world has changed. Let's return for one moment to that dark, dank cave. When we got that moment of spine-tingling uncertainty that something was wrong, what would be the additional or extra information we sought in this bygone era? Likely we would pull as many signals from the sounds we could hear, the landscape we could see, and any difference in the smells in the air. The sound of the grass rustling even though there was no breeze could be the vital clue we needed.

Today, there are plenty of occasions where information seeking is a good and worthwhile strategy. But we have to be careful of the information we consume, too. Not all information is valuable, or even accurate; some sources are purposely hyped up to get a reaction.

Kathryn Buchanan from the Department of Psychology at the University of Essex looked into the emotional reaction of people on social media during the Covid-19 pandemic. She highlighted and suggested that in certain situations – like a pandemic – no additional information will alleviate the feeling of uncertainty.

In addition, in situations where there's an abundance of negative news and people engaging in 'doom-scrolling', it can amplify the concerns already held. In short, those seeking more and more information were also the ones that seemed to display greater anxiety, uncertainty, and be associated with adverse mental health implications.

But what was going on?

Kathryn and her team at the University of Essex put together an experiment. They would randomly assign people to one of three groups.

One group would be exposed to general Covid-19 social media, the second group would be exposed to positive messages: what they called 'Covid-kindness'. The final group was a control group and shown no social media activity during the experiment.[43]

After just two minutes of 'exposure' to these social media messages, the participants were asked to rate their outlook – was it positive or negative, and just how optimistic were they?

In that little time of exposure to negative news, just two minutes, there was a detectable change in the group. They'd developed a far more pessimistic outlook than was seen in the control group. Furthermore, the results seemed to indicate that there was even the possibility that the Covid-kindness group that was exposed to statements such as *This 99-year-old great-grandmother has a lot to celebrate after recovering from COVID-19* gave people a far more positive perspective of the world around them.

In short, Kathryn and her team suggested that it's not so much the delivery method used to consume information but the quality and tone that information takes that has the most effect on our outlook.

The effect of chronic uncertainty

Let's be clear – not all stress is bad. In fact, there is a type of stress, eustress, that is highly beneficial and promotes motivation, performance, and overall well-being.

We experience this type of stress when a gap exists between what we desire and what we have right now. As long as this gap is not too wide, and not too overwhelming, then it has beneficial effects.

But this isn't the type of stress we encounter with uncertainty, particularly if we start thinking about chronic uncertainty.

So, when does chronic uncertainty occur?

Well, let's think this through. In certain cases, uncertainty can be resolved relatively quickly. If we go back to the idea of awaiting test results, this type of uncertainty will be resolved as soon as the test results are released.

While the results may not go the way we wish, and we may feel a wave of negative emotions around the outcome, more than likely, the psychological torture of uncertainty will have been resolved.

In contrast, a quick resolution to uncertainty is rarely available when we think about the future. For one, many things we're unsure and uncertain about take years or even decades to play out. Even then, once we arrive at this future time, yet more innovation and change will already be around us and uncertainty about one thing is simply replaced by uncertainty about another.

This is where uncertainty can become a chronic, rather than an acute, issue, bringing with it a host of unwanted negative side effects.

As neuroscientist, Achim Peters, put it in *Progress in Neurobiology: 'When the acute stress responses turn out to be insufficient for resolving uncertainty, the critical situation may become chronic, and the organism is burdened by "allostatic load"'* (p. 168–88, A Peters et al., 2017).[44]

Allostatic load is not just about uncertainty; it's made up of everything. A cumulative burden of stress from all sources in our environment: diet, exercise, work, and family environment, whether we drink, smoke, and so on.

Make no mistake, uncertainty is a contributor. Suppose you've ever had to await the results of something important, or had your life turned upside down by redundancy announcements, exam grades, divorce, and the like. In that case, you will also know how all-consuming this can be.

The issue is chronic stress and uncertainty aren't just time-consuming or energy-depleting. It affects our mood and our ability to learn as well as our health. Creativity can dip too, and if unresolved, cause burnout.

At a neurobiological level, for us to overcome uncertainty, grow our understanding, or learn anything new, our brains must update.[45] In this regard, our brains make minute-by-minute changes. Our ability to re-shape our brain in this way is often what you hear people refer to as our brain's 'plasticity'. The more adaptable, the more we can adapt.

While our understanding of plasticity has only occurred in the past few decades with advances in neurology, we've understood this at an intuitive level throughout most of human history.

Plato referred to this idea in ancient Greece when he described the brain as a block of wax. Those with softer, more malleable wax, could learn faster and recall more. For those with harder wax, learning ability was diminished.

Let's return to the concept of allostatic load. High allostatic loads, or overload, are shown to be linked to various poor health concerns, such as depression, stroke, and muscle loss.[46] It also diminishes cognition and decision-making ability.

In the short run, many of our adaptive behaviours to uncertainty can be beneficial. But when short-term resolutions are not found, we can get stuck in a maladaptive state,[47] and the proper functioning of key areas of the brain, such as the hippocampus and amygdala that assist in the controlling of mood, among other things, can be compromised. We become far more pessimistic, anxious, and fearful.

Chapter 5

Waves of Innovation

∞

My career in finance started in the summer of 2007 with HSBC. Little did I know at the time, but I was entering the world of finance at the peak of euphoria. Stock markets worldwide were hitting all-time highs and had risen by nearly a hundred per cent since the lows of 2003.

Property prices were soaring off the back of economic promise and relaxing mortgage lending criteria.

Investors in US mortgage firms such as Countrywide had seen tremendous investment returns.

Cheap debt was one of the things fuelling this. Here in the UK, if you were looking to buy a house, not only was there no need for a deposit, but your mortgage could also help buy all that *essential* stuff you'd need on day one.

Northern Rock was one such institution, providing mortgages up to 125 per cent of the value of the house in 2007. Why? Well, because house prices always go up – don't they?

The lesson I was about to learn was to look beneath the noise and hype.

To look behind *first-level thinking* as Howard Marks, founder of Oak Tree Capital, would call it. The type of thinking that is easy and obvious but does not consider knock-on consequences.

While it might sound easy to side-step the hype, drama, and noise, it's not. For one, there is often more than a fraction of truth to the noise and hype we see around us. It's easy to get stuck in it. But rarely is the surface-level noise sufficient to understand a complex environment.

Let's take an example. In 2007, and the years that preceded it, risk in credit markets and stock markets was not only propped up by investors and banks, but also by those professionals who are supposed to be a little more objective and impartial – economists and credit rating agencies.

Take the European Commission. Their economic forecast released in the Autumn of 2007 noted the defaults and the small amount of turmoil going on in America. But it also carried the reassuring tones that everything – at least in the EU – would be all right. After all, the EU and Euro area had started 2007 on a solid note, driven by domestic consumption.

According to this group of experts, the Euro area was in a very good position to 'weather the turmoil in the financial markets' and 'the commission's baseline forecasts assumes that the turbulence will peter out gradually'. 'World GDP (excluding the EU) should ease slightly from 5.6% this year [2007], to 5.3% in 2008 before accelerating again to 5.4% in 2009' (EC Economic Forecast 2007).[48]

The 2008 financial crisis, often referred to as the Great Financial Crisis, ended up being one of the most severe economic shocks to hit the global economy.

When February 2008 came round, the European Commission's forecasts seemed distant history. In the UK, thousands of savers queued for hours, with lines stretching around the block to try to get their money out of failing financial institutions.

The former building society Northern Rock was one of them; with its high exposure to the housing market, it saw its main funding lines cut as lenders' appetites for risk fell.

The pace of this crisis really picked up speed on 15 September 2008 when the American investment bank, Lehman Brothers, collapsed. The ripple effect of this was far and wide. By 2009, countries around the world, with no surface-level connection to the crisis, were also in trouble.

The Queen's visit to the London School of Economics to open a new academic building on 5 November 2008 posed the awkward question that many thought but few dared ask. Surrounded by economists in front of their shiny new building, she questioned them: 'Why did nobody see it coming?'

While the Queen's question was asking *why* it was missed, others were starting to ask far tougher questions. It was here, in the turmoil going on nearly fifteen years ago, that my search for a better understanding of how the world works took flight.

The key thing I would learn is there are forces at play that sit well below the surface and are removed from the daily information that most of us concentrate on. We have become far too reliant on models, and far too short-term in our thinking: both a product of the abundant information world we live in, and our newfound ways of modelling and analysing in almost real-time.

To understand the world, we need to widen our vision considerably. To look forward, we must first look back.

The most important thing that the global financial crisis has done for economic theory is to show that neoclassical economics is not merely wrong, but dangerous.[49] – **Steve Keen**, Economist 2009

It was time to find a better way to think about the world.

The long wave

Nikolai Dmitriyevich Kondratiev, also sometimes spelt Kondratieff, was perhaps the best-known Russian Soviet economist of his day. Kondratiev's fascination was with the natural patterns he'd observed throughout history, which seemed to have a repetition.

He noticed that these cycles or patterns had distinctive phases: faster and slower periods. More than this, they continued despite the minor fluctuations of the business cycle that typically last around ten years.

So far, this book has hopefully done enough to convince you, if you needed convincing in the first place, that the world around us is changing rapidly. But let's start thinking about where this change comes from, and how these cycles Kondratiev uncovered can help us make sense of things going on today.

Kondratiev wasn't the first to notice these longer-term cycles, nor was he the first to suggest that they were the key economic drivers. But he was the first to get this message to a wider audience in his 1925 book *Major Economic Cycles*. He was also among the first to suggest that these waves had a pretty regular pattern and occurred every fifty years or so.

We can find the roots of these waves in significant innovation. Clusters of new technology arise, and a new wave can be seen, spurring on not only new technology, but also, eventually, economic progress, quality of life, and human prosperity.

Just as the rising of the sun brings the opportunity of a new day, the rising of a new paradigm in technological innovation brings the opportunity for the next leg up in the progress of society and the economy.

Let's be clear, the long wave theory Kondratiev suggested is not without its critics. Both in Kondratiev's day and ours. Mainstream economics suggests stability and balance as the causes of progress, not disequilibrium – that's at odds with the long wave theory.

But perhaps the strongest criticism of the long wave approach is the relatively few occurrences we have to examine. In the past 250 years, we have only seen five.

Our modern-day desire to distil everything down to a formula has therefore persuaded us to look at the far shorter cycles around us where we have more data. But in doing so, we cut ourselves off from the rich context of our environment.

Since the late eighteenth century, the world has been driven by a number of key waves or clusters of innovation. As Kondratiev looked back, he could see the first wave in the power of James Watt's steam engine and the Industrial Revolution.

The second wave would then follow with the age of steam and the railways in the early 1800s. Again, followed by a third, the age of steel, electricity, and heavy engineering in the late 1800s.

Working in the 1920s, Kondratiev could already sense that the world was starting its next transition. There were signs that the fourth wave, the age of oil, the automobile, and mass production were underway.

Unfortunately for Kondratiev, there were many changes afoot in the Soviet Union as Joseph Stalin rose to power in a new totalitarian era.

Aside from the economic missteps of Stalin, which led to mass famines, he also exiled or executed those deemed to be political enemies, whose views contradicted his. Kondratiev was one of them.

While we have Kondratiev to thank for observing these long waves of technological progress, uncovering a cause-and-effect relationship was still a long way off. It would be here that Schumpeter, with his concept of 'creative destruction', would come to the fore.

Thinking in eras

Looking back, we can see five distinct waves of innovation since the Industrial Revolution. Each of these lasted multiple decades and supported those early concepts that Kondratiev laid out.

We also see that the information technology age that commenced in the early 1970s is coming to maturity. It was already fifty years old at the time of writing this book. Its 'new ways' of thinking and working are now held as the 'norm' and 'common sense'.

To think of a business starting today with no internet connection, no computer, and no social media seems – well, ridiculous.

But it would be perfectly normal just a few decades before. Tech has become the norm.

But this also likely means that we stand at the start of the sixth wave. Once again, this next wave will transform our society in untold ways and revolutionise how we do things, produce things, and even think – just as the previous ones have.

It will, once again, be highly disruptive – tearing up current structures, and *ways of doing,* calling for entirely new skills.

So, what will be the paradigm-changing technology this time around? Well, we will have to wait and see. But there are a few contenders that lie just on the horizon: for instance, blockchain's ability to create blended realities when combined with AI and AR is certainly one.

But it is important not to focus on just one area. What may make this transformation so powerful and disruptive is that several rising technologies will likely be combined.

With this in mind, we must consider more than just one technology. Here, I would suggest that you do a little reading about blockchain, the metaverse, nanotechnology, personalised medicine, the green energy revolution, and nuclear fusion.

Each of these has the power to meet the definition of a paradigm-shifting technology.

Here too, lies an important point.

Looking into the future is not about predicting as Malthus did, but rather carefully and diligently observing.

It's about being curious about changes and watching the progress of technologies, as well as the rise and fall of trends.

At the heart of each new wave, or paradigm, we find a number of key characteristics. Typically, each new technology, if it's truly to be of the paradigm-shifting kind, must bring decreasing costs, have an almost unlimited supply, as well as provide a platform on which other products and innovators can build. The final requirement is that the new technology is in an area with a widespread presence throughout society. Tick all these boxes, and you have the potential for a new wave.

For these insights, we have to thank the work of numerous researchers over the past few decades who have continued to look at innovation. One such researcher who cannot go unmentioned in this work is Carlota Perez, whose work over the past fifty years has focused on these waves – or what she would call techno-economic-paradigms.

Using common attributes such as decreasing costs, plentiful supply, and a new production system that can be harnessed by others, we can revisit history through a new lens.

At the start of the Industrial Revolution, we find James Watt's steam engine that kick-started it all and allowed for the mechanisation of production in manufacturing – predominantly of textiles.

Watt wasn't precisely the inventor of the steam engine; what he did was innovate it to the point that it was more efficient, more powerful, and could be used in production. Watt's engine, as a result, not only reduced the costs of production through a far faster process, but also created a new platform of technology that others could harness.

New clusters of technologies built up around Watt's engine, from a factory system of production to more efficient ways of transportation, both on land and sea.

It's not just a change in technology and the production of goods or services. The disruption does not stop there – which is a point many overlook.

Technological change brings with it, by necessity, a change in nearly every structure of society.

To understand this, we have to realise that the society we live in today is a result of the technologies we embrace.

From the regulations instituted by policy makers to the physical infrastructure we require. Not to mention our skills and investments, too.

A change in the key technology of the day is, in effect, the reshuffling of society. A displacement in the old way of life that has taken decades to build, and the promise of a new way that is yet to be embraced en masse.

A new paradigm in innovation is not just a new production technique, but a change to the very fabric of the society around us. We, too, have to change with it. That requires a shift in our thinking and understanding. This is far more disruptive than the phrase 'new technological era' perhaps at first sight reveals.

The Industrial Revolution increased productivity through harnessing energy beyond our muscles and the assistance of animals, leading to increases in productivity and prosperity. But we must also acknowledge that doing this ripped up the status quo and the normal 'ways' of doing things.

The famous uprising of the Luddites in Britain, under the command of 'General Ludd', was one such example. People felt threatened, and the future became uncertain, even daunting. In that setting, social unrest broke out, and people tried to maintain and defend the old and familiar way of doing things.

It's not only since the Industrial Revolution that new ideas seen as radical have been attacked and questioned; in fact, we find that this is the more common and typical route that new revolutionary ideas have to take to become accepted. Innovators can have a tough time with it; as Nicholas Klein (1884–1951) put it, 'First they ignore you.

Then they ridicule you. And then they attack you and want to burn you. And then they build monuments to you.'

Examples of this are not hard to find in history.

Take Galileo Galilei, the sixteenth-century astronomer who dared to propose that the current model of understanding about the orbit of the planets was wrong.

At the time the commonly held understanding was based on the Aristotelian geocentric model. This suggested that the Earth was at the centre of the universe and that everything orbited around us. Not only did Aristotle's view have widespread support, but it was also used by the Church and other scientists of the day to support their theories and understanding.

Today, with the advantage of our modern telescopes, we know the earth is not the centre of the universe, and the geocentric theory seems quaint. But at the time? Galileo's challenging theories were not taken seriously.

They threatened the way of thinking. They threatened the common wisdom, and the values society was built on.

Galileo desperately tried to show that his heliocentric theory did not contradict the religious thinking of the time, but alas, the leaders could not see it. And, accused of heresy, he was placed under house arrest for the rest of his life.

Similarly, the observations of the nineteenth-century German-Hungarian physician, Ignaz Semmelweis were a breakthrough in medical hygiene. But once again, they challenged the common wisdom.

Semmelweis made the connection one day in his surgery that there was something more to people catching diseases than could be explained by the miasma theory.

Miasma theory held that foul odours made people ill. This was why people would carry with them 'a pocket full of posies' – to help ward off the poisonous miasma that was believed to bring about cholera.

Semmelweis had an alternative theory that he put to the test in his workplace.

It was not smells that led to contagion but something else. He couldn't quite put his finger on what that something else was, but handwashing seemed to radically change it. Instead of the medical community jumping at the observations of Semmelweis, they condemned him. Eventually, this resulted in Semmelweis suffering a nervous breakdown and being committed to an asylum, where he died.

Over time, just like Galileo, Semmelweis's theory would eventually become a mainstream view. The resistance initially shown demonstrates that shifting paradigms, and seeing things beyond our current way of thinking, is not always easy.

The same is true of the broader economy. The rise of a new era and paradigm threatens the previously established way of life, and the businesses that have built their ways of doing things on them. There is certainly much at stake, and much change afoot.

In today's times, the structures around us are even more complex. Businesses are global phenomena, and today hold considerable levels of debt that can make things even more volatile.

When businesses are complex and heavily indebted, the transition between eras is more than just a change in the way of doing things. It brings with it the genuine risk of financial turmoil and defaults.

The Great Depression of the 1930s was one such turning point. While several factors were behind the events, the rise of mass production was displacing the status quo; taking over from the previous technological era of steel and heavy engineering.

Poor policy decisions of the great 'new deal' in the US likely exacerbated unemployment. However, we should not overlook the changing technology.

Society, and its normal ways, were being uprooted and reformulated to fit the *new way of doing*.

Waves occur gradually (and also have a delay)

It is worth us spending a few minutes considering each of the five waves we've seen since the Industrial Revolution in a little more detail.

One of the first observations we make is that an emerging paradigm-shifting technology does not instantly have a mass impact.

Far from it. Instead, it takes considerable time for this new technology to be refined and eventually adopted by others.

We'll look at how new ideas, innovations, and even paradigms come to be adopted in a later chapter.

For now, let's just bear in mind that the new technology can lie at the fringes, off the radar for most people in society, for years and even decades before it truly becomes mainstream and is seen as 'the norm'.

But when we get to this point, the point of mass adoption, this is when we get some of the most immense upheavals in society. Everything, including the very culture of the world around us, changes.

The Industrial Revolution started taking hold in the early 1770s and ran until around the late 1820s. Those with a keen eye for dates might notice that this is a far shorter time period than many ascribe to it. This is because most historical accounts also group the second wave of innovation (which organised itself around the locomotive, rather than with mechanised production) into the Industrial Revolution.

But there is value in keeping these as distinct periods of time. At least from an understanding of innovation.

Our objective is not one of simply recalling events of history; we must go further if we are to understand how each innovation spurs on its own leg of growth – and a new age.

We should therefore ascribe a warning of being too fanatical about the dates of each wave.

The exact dates for when a wave starts and ends are hard to pinpoint, if not impossible. This is because the technologies of each age overlap in their use. While one may be fading, another is rising.

At what point do we say it has switched?

This inability to precisely measure and date each wave has been a core criticism of the 'wave' theory over the years.

The failure to measure each wave means it cannot be easily measured or elegantly fitted to a formula.

But I argue that instead of it muddying the water, it can provide a certain kind of clarity to our understanding. Our focus shifts from trying to find the precise date something occurs to something far more critical: understanding how and why something happened.

Take the start of the Industrial Revolution as a highlighting point. While James Watts's steam engine is an integral part of this new era, we also have to consider that this single invention was insufficient to transform the cotton industry in Britain by itself.

Instead, it was Watts' engine combined with other corresponding innovations happening at the same time that allowed this wave of machine textile production to occur.

At the time huge progress was made in the spinning and weaving arenas stemming from the Spinning Jenny and the Water Frame at the end of the 1760s.

Here lies the lesson.

Each wave or paradigm shift rarely rests on one single innovation. Rather it harnesses innovations from a number of areas that form a new branch of technological understanding. Trying to ascribe a date, or pinpoint its 'start', is fruitless.

Looking at the First Industrial Revolution, all we can say is a number of key technologies came together in an efficient and useable form as we entered the 1770s.

We also need to be aware that in putting a date on this, while this helps us ascribe an archetype to the period of innovation, we are also cutting off much of the innovation that led to this point.

James Watts was not the first to come up with the concept of the steam engine, but rather took Newcome's steam engine that had been used to pump water from tin mines and made it more efficient, also changing the way it worked so that it could be put to use in the factory setting.

Understanding these long tails of innovation is essential, as it shows the time lag that can be present from an invention or idea being seeded to it finding suitable application in the world.

The Industrial Revolution also provides us with insights into not being too fanatical about when a wave stops or ceases.

The steam engine continued to be used well into the third wave, which eventually brought with it the electric motor that could once again increase production efficiency.

In this sense, the end dates used for waves represent when there was a change in the main driving force of technology, rather than an abrupt end as a date might suggest.

What influences innovation?

Before we end this chapter, it is worth thinking about what influences the direction of innovation.

Is it simply pure chance that there is a breakthrough in one particular area?

Or is there a hidden driving force that increases the chances of a breakthrough in a particular area or field?

While there are undoubtedly chance technological breakthroughs, I will argue that this is not the typical path innovation takes. To understand why, we need to approach this from the entrepreneurial mindset and perspective.

The term 'entrepreneur' I use here is meant in the broadest possible sense to include not just those starting businesses, but also anyone looking to disrupt the status quo to bring about improvements. The rebels, mavericks, and game-changers.

Entrepreneurs and game-changers see the world differently. They notice not only the issues of the day around them, but they also investigate new ways of combining current processes and technologies to overcome the problems others are experiencing.

In this light, we can see the entrepreneurial innovation of the second wave, led mainly by George Stephenson through the reconfiguration of the iron industry and Watt's steam engine. This created a wave of innovation that was centred around transportation. These innovations vastly benefited the cotton industry, as they desperately needed better transportation with increasing volumes of cotton and textiles coming in and out of the factories and ports.

In turn, the locomotive created new problems for other entrepreneurs to tackle. There was an increasing demand for coal and steel. As the knowledge of steel increased during this second wave, the entrepreneurial vision of innovators saw the immense possibilities for this material and refined their processes of production. In a sense, they overcame the issues of the previous wave to spur on new configurations once again, which in turn led to new technologies.

We can see from this process that innovation has its roots firmly in the problems society faces. Today, with the increasing awareness that has been building over the past few decades concerning the environment and climate change, it is little surprise to find so much innovation occurring in this space.

The key issues of our day are the inspiration for change today. Entrepreneurs look at these issues and innovate and create to overcome them. Though they may not necessarily be aware of the impact of their visions and technology, they are quite literally innovating a better world for tomorrow.

While many have researched how waves of innovation come about and transform society, there is reason to come back to an observation Schumpeter made in some of his later works. These observations remain relevant to our understanding today.

He started to understand, as we must too, that innovation is not a simple linear relationship. It is not enough to have a ground-breaking idea or technological breakthrough. If this were the case, then EV cars, which were briefly more popular than combustion engine cars in the early 1900s, would have been the dominant technology. Instead, this EV technology was not valued at the time, raising the interesting question, 'why not?' What's changed today, given their current rise in popularity?

To comprehend change, we need to understand more than just the innovation side. We live in a world that is a complex system with multiple feedback loops.

We need to join up our thinking and look at change in terms of systems – not isolated actors. That would include thinking about trends, capital flows, economic systems, and regulation.

Chapter 6

Joining Up Our Thinking

∞

Shifting geopolitical powers

Above my desk is a corkboard with hundreds of strings stemming from a single picture of Mike Pence standing in a dark suit with a white shirt and blue tie taken on 4 October 2018. His hands clasped over the edge of the lectern that clearly holds the seal of the Vice President of the United States of America.

By itself, the picture is nothing special. I have no personal link to the event, or Mike Pence. But the strings that stem from it on my wall signify a bigger picture than this single speech.

The corkboard is the cumulation of observations and clippings I've collected over the past few years.

Not only watching trends and megatrends but coming to a deeper understanding of how they are connected. I've investigated how they influence the world, society, our individual values, perspectives, and outlooks; understanding how these trends interact and direct disruptive innovation follows.

While we have talked about change from the point of view of speed and magnitude, we have only started to think about change in terms of its direction in the last chapter.

Most people are fully aware that change is occurring. Few, however, have an awareness of its direction and the influences behind it beyond a superficial level. There is a lack in the understanding of how trends interact and can lead to genuinely disruptive change.

We stand on the brink of radical change. A transformation not only of technological progress, but a multi-faceted change that will deeply impact society and the social contract between individuals, businesses, and governments. Change today is coming from nearly every angle you could possibly imagine.

Disruptive technologies of the 1970s heralded the start of the information age and gathered pace in the early 2000s. These have now been embedded into the new *normal* of society, and changes in how we do things can be seen by looking back just a few decades – a past era of printed telephone books and carbon-paper invoice pads.

Businesses that failed to adopt technological change failed to keep pace. The next era will be no less brutal either, potentially even more so.

The backdrop of change today is not just an improvement or change in the technology we use, but it also comes with a series of other highly significant geopolitical, social, environmental, and demographic influences. We should not overlook the shift in the philosophy of culture occurring too.

Let's come back to this picture of Mike Pence. It was taken during a speech on China-US relations. In stark contrast to the calmness of the softly draped American flag and the soft-muted green of the Hudson Institute background stands the language and tone of Mike Pence's speech.

'...using that stolen technology, the Chinese Communist Party is turning plowshares into swords on a massive scale... China now spends as much on its military as the rest of Asia combined, and Beijing has prioritised capabilities to erode America's military advantages – on land, at sea, in the air, and in space' (Vice President Mike Pence's Remarks on the Administration's Policy Towards China, 2018).[50]

For over half an hour, the United States' Vice President laid into the values and ideology of the Chinese people, accusing them of stealing, cheating, and only being in the position they were in because of the economic and cultural might of the US.

The location of this speech that day was no mere coincidence either. The Hudson Institute has, for the best part of eighty years, been a think-tank in long-range forecasting on significant cross-sections of society: economic, security, and international relations. In fact, as a part of his speech, Pence noted the vital role the institute has played in safeguarding national security, peace, and prosperity over the years.

But this speech was less about achievements, and more akin to the declaration of war speeches of eras gone by.

The speech was a wake-up call for many who'd believed President Obama and the media; that the US and China had never been on friendlier footing.

So, what caught my eye on that particular day? Was it the sharp U-turn of sentiment? Was it the curt choice of language that was so undiplomatic? Perhaps. But I suspect it was also something else.

I had never been wholly convinced of the media and the previous administration's view that relations between the US and China had *never been better*. Not when just months before Pence's speech, President Obama had spoken of 'The relationship between the United States and China [as] the most important bilateral relationship of the twenty-first century'.[51] While I agreed with President Obama that the relationship was significant, I didn't share his outlook that it was entirely positive.

Why? Instead of focusing on the rhetoric coming from press meetings, events, and speeches, I had been intensely focused on something else; the trends and megatrends at play. And to my eyes, one of the key developments of the world today is the shifting of global powers, with the US and China at the centre of it.

The US has enjoyed an enviable position for decades being the world's supreme power – and many times during this reign, it had a legitimate claim to also being the world's hyperpower. A title not easily won and infrequently held through modern history.

The concept of a hyperpower goes beyond that of a superpower, occurring only when that one country holds global dominion in every single field: military, cultural, and economic. Hyperpowers are far rarer than superpowers for this very reason.

For the US, that title has already been lost. While it's still perhaps the world's most powerful superpower, it no longer leads in every sphere. In addition, its lead over other nations – particularly China – has been shrinking for some time.

To see this in more than just an intuitive way, we can look to the work of the Lowy Institute, which ranks countries' global power and presence annually through the Asian Power Index. In the 2021 edition, the US made up some lost ground, which was good news for policy makers sitting on American soil. But the uncomfortable fact remained that the researchers at the Lowy Institute in 2021 placed China, not the US, as the global dominant force in two of the eight categories they scored. China was, in the researchers' view, the world leader in their Economic Capabilities and Economic Relationships.[52]

The words of Mike Pence cut straight to the point. The US and China are not partners; they support completely different and incompatible ideological stances.

But there was a greater, unspoken truth in the passion and urgency of these words. The gradual rise of China and the slipping exceptionalism of America were in motion. That's something you won't typically hear a politician or reigning president refer to. It's an embarrassing thing admitting that your nation, well, isn't quite as powerful as it was in its heyday. While not explicitly admitted, it shows up in the campaign slogans such as 'Make America Great Again' under the Trump Administration and 'Build Back Better' under the Biden Administration.

Slogans and dreams aside, history tells us that such transitions in geopolitical powers are rarely frictionless. Quite the opposite, they typically result in war and rising geopolitical tensions.

One of the challenges of this book is to talk about the evolution of trends, and how numerous trends bear down in different ways in situations. In other words, it is not just one factor we need to consider to understand the shift in global power, but numerous. In fact, multiple trends and megatrends combine and are intertwined. Everything is connected.

Books are not the easiest medium to convey this sort of joined-up thinking where multiple trends assert their influence all at once. Books force us to consider one thing at a time. Books are linear; they progress from the first to the last page, leaving an impression that things can be laid out in sequence, separated and analysed in isolation. Ultimately, they can't.

This being said there is still much to learn from looking at the most prominent megatrends individually and becoming familiar with them. But when we think about change, as we see in the shifting of geopolitical powers, we must remember to add them back together and consider the impact of each megatrend on each of the others in play.

Aside from shifting geopolitical power, we have six other key megatrends that we need to consider: climate change, demographics, individual empowerment, resource security, the energy transition, and technological innovation. We'll consider technological innovation and demographics here.

Technological innovation

There are numerous types of innovation that we need to be aware of. For the most part, innovation is not particularly disruptive, even if it brings vast improvements or changes to how we work or live. Examples of this type of *incremental innovation* are all around us.

The development of smartphones in the past ten years is a good example. While the iPhone significantly altered how people thought of mobile communication, it was not disruptive enough to bring about its own paradigm, or age. Instead, it was for our purposes, incremental innovation.

I know that this definition differs from many others. I would suggest that the choice of categorising something as a disruptive or incremental change depends on the timescale with which you view change.

On a shorter timescale, the smartphone is truly disruptive, changing the telecommunication industry and infrastructure with it. On larger time frames, it is part of a bigger innovation cycle – the information technology revolution that started in the 1970s, centering on semiconductors and microchips. In this sense, the iPhone and smartphones of today are a product of this cycle and age.

Other types of innovation are not so benign. They are disruptive because they bring large-scale sweeping changes that separate the world into winners and losers. They open up new branches of possible innovation, new frameworks to work with, and new frameworks that others can then piggy-back off to build on. We have already listed those occurring in the past 250 years, such as the steam engine.

At these points of disruptive change, new technologies emerge, and those who find themselves on the side of the old technology and unable to adapt quickly to the new environment are left behind. They lose market share or slip into far less significant roles.

Such disruptive technologies thankfully occur far less frequently. But when they do occur, they bring new ways of production and new regimes that stand in stark opposition to the current 'norms' of society.

They are disruptive in a second way, too.

They change societal life, the way we think, the values we hold, and we as individuals.

Today, one of the reasons I say we live on the brink of *radical change* is that there are a number of potentially disruptive technologies across several fields that could all come at once – from personalised medicine and nuclear fusion to hyper-automation in the bringing together of artificial intelligence and machine learning. The disruptive technologies of augmented reality and virtual reality have the power to change the essence of what we view as 'the world' as we blur the real and virtual world for the first time. Quantum and Edge computing show promise in bringing seismic shifts in the processing capabilities of computing.

While Hollywood narratives around AI and robots are typically ones that pit us against them, in reality the most likely outcome is collaboration. AI, machine learning, and robotics will take on labour and repetitive tasks, and we humans will be freed to do what we do best – innovate, create, and think outside the box. In short, the relationship and collaboration will likely give us humans superpower-like abilities.

Let's bring this back to the topic of geopolitical power. Think for a moment about how this trend is also intertwined.

Make no mistake; there are significant stakes at risk in being the nation that falls behind in the technology race. While not the sole factor, when we look back through history, it's played an influential role in deciding which nations and states rise in global power and which fall away.

The US knows despite its significant capabilities and world-leading research intuitions focused on many of these disruptive technologies, China is also forging ahead.

In some areas, many believe that China is already winning. The quantum computing race is one such area. It's an area where the Chinese have invested vast amounts of time, energy, and capital to lead the world in artificial intelligence capabilities, intending to remain the global leader in this area over the coming decades.

If the US wishes to remain the global superpower, it should not underestimate these things.

The path of history shows us that the nation that manages to develop and initially 'own' the core disruptive technology of its era gains ever greater levels of power. It gains a first-mover advantage. Of course, this is insufficient to make it the outright greatest. But it sure helps.

If we take a look back, we see this in the UK.

The UK made considerable headway in the 1770s, being the first industrial nation and kicking off the Industrial Revolution. They accomplished this by harnessing the incredible power of James Watt's steam engines and using them in the cotton mills of the day.

By the 1800s, Britain's fabrics were highly sought after worldwide. As demand for British textiles continued to increase, so did the need for cotton to keep these mills running. By the time we reached the 1850s, over half of the US total exports were cotton, with the UK being the primary destination.

Alongside the Industrial Revolution and the booming textile trade, which saw vast amounts of wealth come into Britain, there were also rapid developments in the financial industry. Capital flowed in and was vital in supporting even more innovation.

This potent combination led to an increasingly creative and innovative environment. Under such conditions, it is not surprising to see the next wave of innovation also occur in the UK.

In turn, the UK continued to enjoy its position as the global powerhouse of the world as it led the world into the next wave of innovation. This time it ushered in the age of steam and railways.

Just as with Watt's steam engine, there were a number of locomotives before George Stephenson's 1829 'The Rocket'. But it would be Stephenson that changed the game and brought with it the age of rail and significant changes to the world as we entered the 1830s.

We also notice the competitive advantage a nation holds from being the first to develop such disruptive innovation only sticks for so long.

Complacency can set in, leading to lower levels of innovation, or more attention given to sustaining the core industries of the current age or era, rather than looking to the future of what might be next. In a complacent economy, the technologies that support it become outdated over time compared to others. Other nations not only catch up but overtake.

The age of rail was such a point for the US. The steam locomotive technology was quickly adopted and used, harnessing the power of increasing mobility across a vast geography. Given the size of the US landmass, this brought disproportionate economic benefits over smaller countries such as the UK.

Change doesn't typically happen overnight; such transitions occur over decades. But it happens, nonetheless.

Steel was a vital input in completing the vast railway projects and the growth of pig iron production (the crude intermediate product in the final production of steel) was climbing not just in Britain this time, but in the US and Germany, too.

Steel, electricity, and heavy engineering would be the next wave of disruptive innovation. By most standards, Britain was still leading the way as this age commenced, but not by as much of a lead as in the previous two waves.

In 1875, Britain produced nearly half of the world's pig iron, but the Americans and Germans were catching up, and by the time we got to the start of the 1900s, Britain's global market share had fallen dramatically. When World War I broke out, Britain's share of global production had dropped from over half, to less than a fifth.

While the Great War would significantly impact the future paths of innovation, particularly in the passing of global power from Britain and Germany to the US, it would also highlight the British steel industry's failure to keep pace with the technology of the Americans. Even before the 1900s, signs of complacency and a reluctance to upgrade the manufacturing techniques of British steel are visible, but perhaps most starkly in the fact that America was able to manufacture and sell their steel far cheaper.

The passing of power between global powers and the involvement of innovation and technological development brings us back to the very start of this chapter. It also serves as the backdrop for why the US will more than likely fight to keep its power in the world and simultaneously try to slow the technological progress of the Chinese.

Once again, we must bring in other megatrends to gain a better picture. This time, we need to bring in demographics.

Demographics

Japan is often referred to as the super-aged society, holding first place in the oldest society awards. China, it is often joked, will be the country that will become 'old, long before it becomes rich'. That's not a joke that goes down well in China, which already sees the last one hundred years as a century of humiliation.

An ageing society can cause nations significant problems. But that trend might be about to change, or at least ease-off a little for a few countries. That's the bet that China is making. Perhaps automation can replace human labour?

Coming back to Japan, its population is so old today that nearly thirty per cent of its people are over the age of 65. Furthermore, it's a country where the population is expected to shrink significantly over the coming decades, as births don't keep up with deaths. Most modern predictions take the population of 126 million in 2021 and see this falling to around 88 million by 2065.[53]

These shifts cause some unique challenges to the Japanese government, as well as for the towns and cities of the country. This trend is nothing particularly new for Japan; their demographic problems started to make headlines in the 1990s when their baby boomer generation after the Second World War, kept failing to maintain fertility rates above the minimum required 2.1 replacement level.

In recent years, Japan has become a leading nation in robotics as one solution to try and maintain economic productivity in the face of a falling labour pool. In addition, the government and certain towns have launched 'Cash for Kids' style initiatives to try and at least encourage the current family-age generation to have more children.

The latest round in this saw the town of Sado in the Niigata Prefecture promising want-to-be parents two million yen for having a third child – and any subsequent child after that. The rationale was simple: government stimulus was needed after decades of fertility well below the replacement rate.

While this might sound extreme, it's not without its reason. The socioeconomic toll of a shrinking society comes with a heavy burden.

That said, Japan has been relatively successful in maintaining its standard of living. Japan's fall from being an economic powerhouse in the early 1990s is partly due to this demographic issue. The falling population has not just brought about fewer hands to do the work, but far less innovation, too.

It would be easy to think that this ageing demographic issue is only a Japanese one. But we could add China in here too. Even this would miss the point that this is a global phenomenon. Very few countries around the world have what would be traditionally called 'good demographics'. India's demographics, with a large base of young, working-age people, and a smaller population of older, dependent-age people at the top is a rarity today.

The world population reached one billion people after more than fifty thousand years. By the 1960s, the world's population had reached three billion; six billion by 2000, and it is forecasted to stretch to nine billion by 2037. As the birth rate increased, so did that wider base of working-age people.

The global growth rate is slowing dramatically, and the population is ageing faster than ever. With this shift in demography, governments are confronted with issues they've never had to navigate before and, in many cases, problems they've not anticipated.

Let's think of this in terms of the dependence ratio. While this may sound daunting, the dependency ratio is simply the number of non-working age people compared to the number in work.

As such, it indicates the economic pressure on working-age people to support those who are not, in addition to themselves. Over the past few years, many developed nations have seen moves by their governments to increase and encourage individuals to take out private pensions, a move based on the growing understanding that many state pensions, like the UK's, are simply funded by receipts from taxes. However, in the future, as the dependency increases, such programmes will become frightfully more expensive and burdensome on the working population.

It's not just pensions; in many countries, existing institutional and social systems are unsuitable for ageing populations and changing demographics.

Low birth rates and longer life expectancies create several challenges for a nation, including reduced productivity, increasing health care expenditure, and rising costs of the social safety net. An ageing population puts the public sector under financial pressure. Today, the baby boomers are retiring and, with an increased lifespan, the demographics are shifting.

Healthcare institutions worldwide are becoming increasingly concerned about dealing with ageing populations.

Take the US. Its age structure is changing dramatically. The impact of previous drops in fertility and increased life expectancy can harm the economy's performance and the long-term viability of government entitlement programmes – not to mention a potential change in consumer consumption. By 2060, the population of the United States is expected to increase by 79 million people, from around 326 million in 2018. The home care industry in the United States is anticipated to grow from $100 billion in 2016 to $225 billion by 2024, owing to an ageing population.[54]

It's not just natural demographic changes. Population control policies can lead to ageing problems too, as seen in empirical data from China. By 2026, China's elderly population could number more than 300 million, increasing to 400 million by 2041.[55]

Looking at China, we can't fail to notice that family planning programmes have irreversibly harmed the demographic structure during the last half-century. In 2016, China ended its 'one-child policy' and moved to limit couples to two children instead. This policy was originally implemented to address a rapidly deteriorating demographic situation that poses a slew of social and economic issues. The new government programme aims to help elevate this and bring down the costs of educational resources.[56]

Beyond the simple change in the median age of a population, the consumer habits and overall level of spending change too.

According to Experian research, annual expenditures and pre-tax income are 'hump-shaped' across the typical lifespan. With the lowest levels for those under 25 years old, rising to the greatest levels for those 45–54 years old as incomes increase, and then falling once again.

Evidence shows that as people age, their spending patterns change, with a more significant emphasis on health-related services as we get older.

With more people living longer lives, the employment ratio is projected to decline. Ageing offers a clear concern. The ageing of the population will lower many economies' growth rates. In addition, higher taxation on company earnings and family income from savings, such as dividends, interest, and capital gains, would be necessary to fund an older population's increased pension and health benefits. Such taxes would add to the economy's burden and slow its growth.[57]

This is where we need to bring the story of this chapter full circle. It highlights why the race to develop new technologies and gain the competitive advantage of being the leader in that field is becoming so important to China and the US. However, we should not leave Europe out once again.

In times gone by, countries needed more people not only for taxes to support state systems, but also to fight wars. But there is reason to suggest that things like an increasing dependency ratio may not be as strong a predictor of economic hardship as it once was.

If technology can replace the labour of humans, then productivity need not slump as much. Still, there are sweeping changes that such a shift would bring. Unlike a human workforce that gets paid and spends in the economy, machines and software don't bring the same spending patterns. While the demographic production problem might be overcome by it, it brings significant change. Being one of the first to embed labour-saving technology into an economy is also a significant advantage. China wants to win this race.

There is another threat in this demographic perspective for countries. China is likely to lose its status as the most populous country in the world over the coming years. Today, India and China have very similar population numbers. But India has one key advantage. Its population is far younger, with an average age of just 28.4 years. Compare this to China where the average jumps up to 38.4 years.

India's economy might be just a fraction of China's and the United States', but its demographics are far better. The gap, while moving slowly, is likely to close significantly.

Chapter 7

Dipping Below the Noise

∞

So far, you could be forgiven for thinking that successfully seeing all these things around you would take endless time, effort, and energy. But you'd be wrong.

While you may need to increase your level of curiosity and develop a detective-like interest in the world around you, you do not need to consume ever more information to be good at it. Quite the opposite.

The framework I provide in this book will set you on the right path. Core to this is knowing where to look, understanding the patterns of change, and learning to dip below the noise. We will look at all of these approaches in this chapter.

When we come to the topic of trends, most people know they are out there. Beyond that, many have little idea how to spot them or follow them. Trends in most people's minds have a mysterious quality that makes them appear as if they come from nowhere and vanish just as quickly. With this illusion in place, it is little surprise that most people think that only those with the highest level of intuition can spot them as they emerge. But if one thing about trends is true, it's that they always bubble under the surface for a long time before they fully emerge. It is this time delay and incubation period that gives us time to not only spot them, but also to watch their development, and even ready ourselves for their arrival.

Most of this book is concerned with megatrends. A type of trend that typically lasts decades and holds influence over the core pillars of the world around us: technology, social structure, the environment, geopolitics, and demographics.

They can build in the background before most become aware of them. Megatrends are very slow-moving, and once they get going, they become a force to be reckoned with.

The concept of the *megatrend* was first introduced in the 1980s in a book with the same name, written by the late John Naisbitt. John's work highlighted the need to listen very carefully to the underlying trends and movements of the world.

By doing so, not only could you start to tease out some of the more profound changes occurring, but you could also begin to build insight into what you should be studying, where you might want to work, and what skills to pursue.

Let's start with a simple observation. The data we take in greatly affects our perceptions of the world. Therefore, *how* we approach data, and *what* we consume should be highly questioned.

Over the past couple of decades, data has increased exponentially. So how do we become better at listening to the changes around us in a world of data excess? One secret is to cut out the amount of information you consume. Yes. Reduce it.

I'm not talking about cutting yourself off from everything – that won't help either. That's a step too far. But there is a middle ground. You can afford to cut out a lot of the breaking news, hyped-up mass media, and social media speculation with little loss of understanding. In fact, understanding could increase if you do.

Hyped-up, sensationalist media is a bit like eating a steady junk-food diet. It feels good at first, but then the composition of low-quality calories and little to no nutritional value soon catches up. Over time, many people report feeling tired, bloated, and sluggish. The same thing happens when your information diet is one of just fast-paced media.

So, if we're not going to be upping our information content, what will we be doing?

In the previous chapter, we started to think about some of the major trends going on, how these interact with the global powers of the day, and where innovation cycles fit in.

These trends offer an extremely valuable source of slow-moving data. And slow-moving means that it's not all-consuming, leaving you more time to be curious about everything around you, such as Tamagotchis in the 1990s.

Is my Tamagotchi alive?

In the late 1990s, nearly every kid in the western world was exposed to the radical, attention-consuming Tamagotchi. Yep, including the twelve-year-old me. I can confirm that there was something addictive about them.

But why? What did they do that toys before didn't? At its core, it was simply a small plastic egg-shaped toy with only three buttons and a pixelated outline of a digital creature – the Tamagotchi.

To understand its addictive appeal, we need to reflect on the time period. While it was only a couple of decades ago, it was still some ten years until the iPhone would launch. Computers were common, but not everywhere, and AI was still, for most people, an abstract idea that only rested in Sci-Fi movies.

However, out in Japan, there was a man named Akihiro Yokoi. As the story goes, Yokoi loved animals, but not only this, he was also the president of the Japanese firm 'Wiz toys'. As luck would have it, he was in charge of handheld products. The list of the pets that Yokoi had was long.

From the common dogs and cats, to parrots, chameleons, and turtles. Yokoi's breakthrough wasn't, as you might think, to be the first person to construct a digital pet. There were already PC games that allowed you to do this, and even other handheld devices that gave you a virtual dog or cat.

Where Yokoi struck gold was in the fact that the Tamagotchi could easily die.

Owning a pet isn't just about checking in on it every now and again. Much of pet ownership is a right pain in the arse. It was this realism that he wanted to bring to the plastic, three-buttoned egg. It meant that kids simply couldn’t put it down. If they did, you could come back and find that you hadn't cleaned up the digital poop and your Tamagotchi was no more.

Schools started to notice that kids were bringing these things to class, who were routinely checking it to make sure it didn't need food, a drink, or cleaning. In these early models – before schools started banning them and parents were given the task of caring for them throughout the school day – there was no pause button. That would come much later.

As is with most kids’ toys, there is always space for the next brightest shiny thing, and the Tamagotchi’s end would eventually come. A new toy would surpass it and capture the minds of the youth in another way.

But Yokoi’s Tamagotchi did well. It had captured the attention of the world. Parents had queued up for hours around the block to try and get one, and in total, they'd sold just under one hundred million Tamagotchis. Funerals were even held for many that died.

Was the Tamagotchi really a trend? Come on!

Before we’re too quick to dismiss the long-forgotten Tamagotchi as just a fad, let’s discuss this in a bit more detail.

What's a trend anyway?

Before we go much further, it might help to clarify what a trend is.

The word 'trend' has been around for quite some time, and perhaps originated from the old English word 'trendan' which meant to revolve or rotate. By the time we get to the sixteenth century, we start to find evidence of the verb being used to describe when something turns in a specific direction.

While we could continue to home in on a more precise definition, this would likely only complicate things. 'Turning in a specific direction' is simple and accurate enough for our use.

Our job, therefore, is to become more attuned to *what* is turning, and better understand in which direction it is moving.

We need only look to human behaviour for the signals of most trends. When we start to see changes in how humans behave and societies structure themselves, we begin to get an excellent and reliable indication that there is more to understand.

With this in mind, let's come back to the Tamagotchi.

While it's undoubtedly clear that the Tamagotchi is not a megatrend by itself, we should not so quickly dismiss everything about it as a fad. Even though by most definitions of a fad, it fits well: a temporary move, change, or mania.

This is where we need to dip further below the noise. If we think about this more carefully, we would be forced to admit that while the Tamagotchi took the market by storm, it vanished as quickly as it arrived. Today, outside of a few die-hard fan clubs, the toy is almost forgotten globally. Multiple age groups will have no memory, recollection, or knowledge of it.

That said, I'm going to suggest that the Tamagotchi was, while not a trend itself, part of a bigger trend that has been at play ever since. It is one that has been building momentum and is set to become a megatrend – affecting cultural attitudes and social behaviour on a global scale.

The technology that Yokoi used, while primitive by today's standards, interacted with the user like few toys had until this point.

It brought a certain aliveness to the plastic. While it was clear to all that the toy was not alive in the sense a real dog or cat was, it also felt somehow not entirely or distinctly a computer. It was far more alive than that.

The Tamagotchi signalled the blurring of the lines between virtual and physical worlds, and our relationships with non-living things.

Technology today is almost unrecognizable compared to the primitive nature on display in the mid-1990s. The blurring of these lines continues with the rise of the metaverse, robotics, and AI just around the corner.

Gradual change

One theme you will find running through this entire book is that change is not the ultra-rapid process many people perceive it to be.

Sure, change can be fast at times, and overall, change is getting faster with the aid of technology. But much of our perception of the speed of change comes back to our lack of awareness of the trends in place. Our failure to see them while they are merely bubbling beneath the surface.

Kodak

Kodak, following its launch, dominated the photographic industry in the US. By the mid-1970s, it was at its peak, commanding ninety per cent of the film market, and nearly as much of the camera market. It simply could do no wrong.

George Eastman, born in 1854 in New York, launched Eastman Kodak in 1880, which would become one of the world's largest companies.

By 1984, the first signs of its falling dominance in the new competitive landscape were visible. Kodak lost its bid on home soil to be the official sponsor of the Los Angeles Olympic games, losing out to its growing rival Fuji, which in turn gave the Japanese firm a way into the US market (something they'd been looking to do for some time).

As 2011 came around, Kodak was in serious trouble. The CEO, Antonio Perez, was forced to start selling off patents as investors began to worry about the rate at which the company was eating its way through its cash reserves. To make matters worse, it was also dropped from the S&P 500 stock index, a US-based index of America's 500 largest companies.

But Perez was no pushover. He was well-qualified and a well-experienced lead. Before joining Kodak, he'd worked at Hewlett Packard as corporate vice president. In addition, he had experience in electronic engineering, marketing, and business, an MBA from the world-famous INSEAD, and an honorary doctorate from the University of Rochester. If this was not enough, he'd built experience helping large investment firms navigate technological disruption.

But management had completely misjudged the oncoming digitalization trend in the photographic world way before Perez's hiring. They had not taken the oncoming digital trend seriously. When the pivot came, it was too little too late.

On the 19 January 2012, the Kodak company filed for bankruptcy.

What makes this even more surprising is it was Kodak's engineer, Steven Sasson, who developed the first digital camera during his time at Kodak in 1975.

Trends are not ultra-rapid events. But we should not mistake their slow pace of change for weakness. We underestimate their power at our peril. What they typically lack in speed, they make up for in persistence and formidability. When in full swing, little that stands in their way survives.

The digital trend in photography would take thirty-six years from its conception to the point it would take out the company that conceived it.

While the Kodak story is famous, it is not the exception. Time and time again, we find situations where people are unaware of change, and the direction it takes things. When this happens, and we become unaware of the landscape we live in, it can have dramatic effects.

Blockbuster, the video rental business founded in 1985 in Dallas, Texas, is another case in point.

As the video and DVD business grew, Blockbuster took on the international market and won. Its outlets located around the globe, including the Pacific, Europe, and South America.

Around 2000, Blockbuster was given the opportunity to acquire a new upstart company. This company operated in the same space as Blockbuster but saw the future not in physical videotapes and DVDs, but on the internet. The company, called Netflix, would come with a modest price tag of $50 million.

Reed Hasting, the co-founder of Netflix, however, was laughed out of the room. After all, what did the mighty Blockbuster need with a start-up like Netflix? Blockbuster knew what they were doing!

A few years later and the rapid removal of Blockbuster from the highstreets worldwide was yet again another indication of a growing trend in place.

I could keep going with the business examples, and it's not just giants like Kodak, Blockbuster, or Blackberry. This process of technological change impacts every industry, every department, every home, and every college.

Sometimes we never know the opportunities we pass by because we don't see the signs of change. Take the alleged story of Dick Rowe at Deca Records, who is said to have turned down The Beatles in 1962. Or to bring this back to you, imagine the degree or course you would have done if only you had known then what you do now.

I am not suggesting that we can gain perfect foresight. But as the saying goes, *it is better to be vaguely right, than precisely wrong.*

Weak signals and knowing where to look

To get better at seeing the wider picture around us, we need to widen our field of vision.

Within the professional world of foresight practice, this would typically be referred to as scanning, which is pretty much what the word suggests – looking intently at what's changing and being more aware and observant.

Environmental scanning as a concept dates back to research done by Francis Joseph Aguilar in the 1960s at Columbia University, which became popular in the business and consulting world in the 1970s and 1980s.

In the business sense, environmental scanning is focused on trying to find the forces outside of the organization's control, but that nonetheless have an impact. Blockbuster and Kodak would have done well to look at the force of digitalisation, and the role this might take, thinking about outcomes in terms of scenarios.

Instead of looking at the current environment and trying to tease out the forces at play, another technique that allows people to look to the future is horizon scanning. Those who support horizon scanning over environmental scanning typically do so because they feel that the focus of environmental scanning – trying to find factors already at play – is too short-term. It is focused on the world already here, rather than the world that might be in the future.

While this may seem to be no more than semantics and word play, there is something in this that we can learn from.

Horizon scanners look for 'weak signals'. These are areas that many people may have little understanding of or even an awareness of its existence. Their approach is not to look at the mainstream developments, but to look for emerging forces.[58]

Thankfully, we do not need to get caught up in the ins and outs of differences between these schools of thought. Our concern is for the practical application and how these concepts can assist us in our pursuits.

To keep it simple, the general idea behind *scanning* is just that – scanning the periphery for what might be coming and what's driving change right now.

We want to become aware of the weak signals or the very early trends starting that might develop over the coming years. In this way, weak signals supplement trend analysis and they can be used to expand on alternative futures. Additionally, we also want to consider the trends and megatrends in play right now.

Overall, we want to become far more aware of the possibilities, changes, and developments we can see going on around us now and think through what these mean in terms of a new future.

Essentially, it's upping our attention and observation. When we do this and consider possible futures, we become more attuned to the overall zeitgeist – the spirit of the age. We also become less susceptible or blindsided by change.

The other benefit this brings is an awareness of the things you see, and how you approach new information. Does the new information fit or contradict what you think you know?

When trends end

So far, we have talked about trends as if they continue forever. While some can last multi-centuries such as the world's urbanisation, trends typically end at some point. They can also slow, speed up, and pause.

It is no secret that Americans have had an enduring love affair[59] with their cars, trucks, and automobiles for decades. It makes sense too; in a country with a landmass such as the USA, it pays dividends to be mobile.

But the relationship with their cars is far more than practical. They've elevated their social status to play central roles in films and TV series over the years. What would the 1980s TV drama Knight Rider be without 'KITT' the customised 1982 Pontiac Firebird?

Or for that matter, what would films such as *Gone In Sixty Seconds*, or *James Bond* be without their cars? The list goes on.

At first glance, the figures suggest that this trend – the American love affair with cars – is far from peaking.

The data suggests that the number of short-wheelbase light duty vehicles put out by the US Bureau of Transportation Statistics[60] is going up nicely.

In 2020 there were some 193 million such vehicles registered in the US. This went up from just 61 million in 1960 using the same database.

But remember that sometimes we have to be a little more curious about data. We have to look behind the headline. What else do we know about the US? What other trends are in play? How about the number of households and people of driving age?

In 2013, Michael Sivak at the University of Michigan Transportation Research Institute asked a similar question: what was happening to car ownership levels in the US? The conclusion of his research looked at ownership over the period 1984 to 2011 and found it declined just before 2008. Although he was quick to point out, this did coincide with one of the biggest recessions in history.

But what did Sivak observe in this short research paper titled 'Has Motorization in the US Peaked?'.[61]

Calculating both the number of light-duty vehicles along with the number of households, Sivak concluded that the average number of cars registered per household rose steadily from 1.84 cars per household to 2.05 between 1984 and 2005.

Since this peak, it's started to fall.

He pointed to two other trends that might explain why the average number of registered cars is dipping and why the American love affair with the car might be ending. There was an increase in the percentage of people using public transport and telecommuting – what we'd commonly refer to as remote working today.

Dig a little deeper and we also see that the average age of the person buying the car was going up significantly.

This changing trend was not just taking place in America, but in Europe, too.

The UK analysis by the Commission on Travel Demand noticed the same thing: there are fewer young people driving today than in previous generations. In fact, younger people were not travelling as much or as far. Day-to-day life was remaining far closer to home. As for the number of young adults with driving licences, this was on the decline, too. In 2018, researchers from The Centre for Transport & Society from the University of Bristol, and the Transport Studies Unit working out of the University of Oxford, presented their findings. While there were a few financial reasons for young adults not taking up driving, there were a host of other reasons too, including increasing urbanisation, starting families later, and the rapid rise of digital socialisation.[62]

Chapter 8

Transitions Can Be Painful

∞

We've covered a lot of ground and built up some core concepts. But it's now time to turn our attention to why transitions between eras and ages can be so painful to us as individuals, and why there is so much disruption created when two technological paradigms clash.

In describing the waves of innovation, we have talked about two different paces of change: the slower pace of change coming from *incremental innovation*, and the far faster pace of change stemming from *disruptive innovation*.

While you will find many authors and commentators using the phrase *disruptive innovation* for nearly everything under the sun, this book uses it far less liberally.

In fact, we only use the term *disruptive innovation* to specifically talk of the paradigm-changing type of innovation that occurs in waves, every fifty years or so. The periods that change the way everything is done and that have the power to change the status quo.

As we saw in the Kodak and Blockbuster examples, there is a crucial phase of transition in which the two systems clash: the fading of the old innovation system, and the rising of the new. At these points, long-standing industries that have been the bellwethers of the market can see slow, gradual decline where they fail to update and adapt. While other companies, often fresh young faces, emerge.

But we need to look closer at the process of change to understand why the transition periods can be disruptive. The idea that there are fast and slow periods is helpful but not the complete picture.

To gain a better understanding, we need to see the world differently.

We need to think of it in layers. Layers such as the business layer, or the cultural layer.

But why are layers important? Simply because not all layers update at the same time, and they also update at very different speeds.

The fastest layers move very quickly, perhaps updating seasonally; in contrast, the slowest layers move exceptionally slowly, updating only every few millennia.

While this may initially seem complicated, most people find that when they step back, it's far more intuitive than it first sounds.

The main point to pull from this is that disruptions and transitions are not smooth events. A paradigm shift in technology, or a shift in the core philosophy of culture, will disrupt nearly all the other layers too.

Let's think about this from a view of the ultra-fast layer of fashion, which can go through annual or even seasonal changes. This may revolve around colours, fabrics, and cuts of clothing.

But the influence on this layer is not just the designer's tastes. It also comes from shifts in other layers – such as core consumer values and fabric technology.

Athleisure, derived from the words *athletic* and *leisure*, is a great example. A movement that combines new fashion trends, new materials, and changes in society, such as the body-positive culture.

At the other end of the spectrum, the ultra-slow changing layers – we have the environment. The natural environment changes at much slower speeds: it operates not in years or decades, but often millennia.

Viewing change in this timeframe, we can see that even the world's current configuration is just a temporary phase.

Two hundred million years ago, the shape of the world's landmass was very different. It didn't look as it does on maps today, it was instead formed of a single supercontinent called Pangea.

Pangea wasn't even the first supercontinent; there have been several before in the Earth's history and there will be more.

Between these two extremes, we also find other vital layers that update at differing speeds – some slow, some fast.

Feedback loops between the layers exist too. When change occurs in one layer, it seeds change in the others.

So, what are these layers? In between the super-fast changing pace of fashion and the super slow pace of the natural environment, Stewart Brand, in his book, *The Clock of The Long Now*, identifies several others: business, infrastructure, regulation, and cultural layers – running in order from fastest to slowest speeds of change.

Businesses and infrastructure typically update faster than regulation. And in turn, regulation updates faster than culture.

As you move along the spectrum of these layers, it is not just their speed that changes – but also their impact. Changes in the very slow-moving environment are more impactful than changes in the business or fashion layers.

The error in our thinking

Most people miss the fact that these layers of the world around us have different speeds of change. In fact, it would probably be fair to say most people don't think of the world in this way at all.

Instead, people typically see change as a steady, all-encompassing process.

From this perspective, when change occurs in one layer, the assumption is that everything moves as one, in some synchronicity – a carefully orchestrated dance.

But viewing the world in this way leads us to some serious miscalculations. We expect calm, orderly change, and instead we get disorder.

Also, when we expect changes to our lives to occur smoothly, we become underprepared for the turbulence. This adds to the levels of uncertainty that we experience.

At its worst, it can divide populations and sections of the economy.

Suppose a change originates from the cultural values of society. In that case, people start asking why haven't businesses, infrastructures, and regulations changed with it? Are they stalling? Are they unwilling to change?

In these situations, people quickly start screaming that more must be done to get others to change – and faster. While the frustration they are feeling is genuine, the illusion that everything can change overnight is just that – an illusion.

Look around today, turn on the news, and you will see this happening.

As the gaps between layers grow, a kind of disequilibrium occurs. While it is the perfect breeding ground for ground-shaking innovation, it is also the breeding ground of uncertainty, anxiety, and pessimism.

And as we looked at in an earlier chapter, chronic stress can even lead to physiological changes in our brains: the atrophy of the hippocampus,[63] a region of the brain heavily involved in learning and memory.[64] Such an environment can physically change us when not anticipated or expected.

Innovation brings direction change

Moving beyond the layers of change, we also need to think about the direction of change.

We have already looked at the framework of innovation cycles. We've built an understanding that every forty to sixty years or so a truly disruptive wave of innovation brings with it a new era. But a new era really codes for a change of direction.

Direction changes at the global scale are something that we don't frequently come across in our day-to-day life experiences. This is partly because such global changes only show up every few decades.

But we can look to our personal lives for examples that resonate. In our own lives, either personally or through the people we know, we will have seen times of major transitional shift. This can show up in events such as losing a loved one, narrowly escaping death, divorce, starting a new business, emigrating to a new country, losing a job, having children, and so on.

These fundamental life transitions have parallels with the major shifts that can occur on the global stage when we go through paradigm-shifting change.

The most dramatic changes in history have changed the direction of progress. Take the shift from being a nomadic hunter-gatherer. A time when we would roam around in tribes of eighty or so people, foraging and hunting.

The seismic change was to come when they changed direction. They started cultivating edible plants, which required them to stay put in one place. Suddenly a new and radically different social environment was created. With it came new possibilities, but also new challenges and issues.

Likewise is the change that occurred from the Agrarian Age to the Industrial.

The same applies to each wave we have seen in the past two centuries.

Truly disruptive innovation takes us on new paths. It's very different from the incremental innovation that we're used to. Disruptive innovation is not smooth, it's rarely expected, and it forcefully changes the status quo.

To truly understand disruptive innovation, we must realize that this is not a consistent process.

In contrast to incremental innovation, which makes small continuous changes, disruptive innovation is different. It clusters with other technologies, builds like a pressure cooker, and then jumps forward, creating an imbalance in the layers of the world around us, requiring us to rapidly change our approach to life.

This is why the paradigm-shifting type of innovation, which leads to the transitions this book talks of, comes in waves and shakes the foundations of our society.

It changes the philosophy of the culture around us. The belief systems, the way we do things, how we interact with each other, and what we expect from one another. In other words, each wave not only changes our businesses and infrastructure, but us, too.

As outlined in earlier chapters, we have seen five waves since the Industrial Revolution.

The last one, the information technology revolution, is reaching maturity. This is not to say that the information technology age is over. Far from it. But rather, its benefits have been mass adopted.

The next wave of change is already rising. Building on the information technology wave we have just been through, the next wave will bring a blending of virtual and physical worlds, and mass automation.

Global consulting firms such as McKinsey & Co. have projected that the next ten years will see unprecedented levels of re-skilling and unemployment. As companies fully embrace the technological abilities around us, the projection stands that at least thirty per cent of daily tasks in around six out of ten jobs could be done more efficiently by technology.[65]

This is the kind of direction-changing disruption that changes the status quo significantly.

If we look to other times of change, we can see why we need to be aware of what's going on. Wales, the country I live in, had a massive economic reliance on coal mining.

In some areas, entire villages depended on the industry for work and their livelihoods. At its peak in the 1920s, the UK coal mining industry employed 1.1 million people. By 2005, that number had declined to just six thousand.[66]

Professor Steve Fothergill at Sheffield Hallam University points out that the areas hit the hardest would take decades to see any real effect from regeneration projects.

Re-skilling, building new industries, and finding displaced workers new jobs was a painful process for many mining towns.[67]

But what is even more illuminating is that this was a time when the UK, on aggregate, was seeing unemployment levels fall and a surge in the number of people in jobs. So, why didn't the old mining towns simply bounce back and switch jobs?

In part it was their location. But it was also because the skill set of the coal miner was suddenly not desired.

The bottom line is change, in any format, is uncomfortable. Most people don't like it.

Even if we become aware of changes occurring and we give ourselves a chance to change before it's too late, there is an inertia at a cognitive level to changing.

Whether this change is to do with the industry we work in, or the technology we use. The familiar just feels safer.

Change aversion is not just applicable to large-scale events either – it shows up in people's negative reactions to almost anything *new*.

The launch of the iPhone highlighted this with its revolutionary button-free design. The touch screen would become an outright success, and a defining feature of smartphones to come.

But consumers' initial reactions to Apple's plans?

It was hardly positive. They thought Apple had lost the plot. '[I]t seems no one told Apple just how bad of an idea touch screen buttons are' and 'I'm sticking with my old phone – it's way better than this'.[68]

Change is hard

Let's start tying these ideas together. We've been talking about the different speeds of change in different layers of the world and the increased pace of change when new waves of *disruptive innovation* occur.

Grace Hopper might not be a name you're overly familiar with, but you should be. She was undoubtedly a pioneering mind in the field of computer science, and the person behind the quote that cuts to the heart of our inertia to change: 'the most dangerous phrase in the English language is "*we've always done it this way*"'.

To give her full title, Rear Admiral Grace Hopper broke the mould. She was not only a pioneering female computer programmer (when there simply weren't any female computer programmers), but she also had an unnatural level of observation. She saw things others didn't.

'We've always done it this way' is, unfortunately, one of the biggest traps of human nature.

Habits, we know all too well, are hard to break. We like routines. The status quo is comfortable. To change is painful because, at its heart, it involves loss. Loss of the current way of doing things, the relaxed way of doing things, and the way you know how to do things.

Bringing this back to transitions and the different rates of change that we see in the world, particularly between the faster changing economy and the slower changing society, we have two options: change on our own terms, before we need to, or change when we have to. Let's be clear, neither is an easy choice to make.

To understand why, we need to think about the psychology of change and bring some behavioural insights to the table.

First, let's consider just how bad most of us are at self-directed change. Take New Year's resolutions as an example.

Typically, as the new year approaches, for around half of the population it is the right time to clean the slate and correct some of the bad habits they've let slip into their lives. They see it as the time to work on things they've been meaning to for a while – but haven't.

A study conducted by two researchers from the University of Scranton in the US, titled 'The Resolution Solution',[69] found that those sticking to their New Year's resolutions were just a tiny minority. Even after just one week, thirty per cent had already dropped off. Once we look further out, that number grew significantly.

But why? These were things that people wanted to achieve for themselves. Why didn't they?

The simple fact is that change isn't easy, even when you want it.

The author of the book *The Power to Change*, Campbell Macpherson, suggests that we think about change in a quadrant or matrix. In this, we can separate change into two halves. Is the change we're thinking of big or small? Secondly, is this something we're initiating, or are these changes being externally forced upon us?

Macpherson suggests that depending on the size of the change and where the motivation is coming from, our experience of change changes with it.

We can easily cope with small changes, whether self-driven or externally forced. On the whole, these changes are commonplace and easy to navigate. It could be something simple like changing where you park or deciding to drink more water each day.

But when we come to changes that bring far more impact on our lives, it suddenly gets far more complicated. Change is no longer all that easy. These changes come with massive implications for our life.

On the self-motivated side, do we change jobs, houses, or get married?

On the externally influenced side: we get fired, lose our spouse, or have to move locations because war, famine, or climate change dictates it.

Change at this level is not only more impactful, but far more challenging for us to cope with.

At the heart of this is the fact that habits are hardwired into our neurology. These habits form shortcuts that make it easier to make decisions, which from the brain's perspective means life is less energy-intensive and, therefore, our preferred option.

Let's make one thing clear. Habits aren't always bad. Good habits can help us navigate life, provide us with a certain level of structure, and can help us maintain focus on the areas of life that we deem essential.

They make you put your keys in the same place every time you walk in through the door, so you know where they are when you need them in a rush. They make it the default to brush your teeth before bed, and again when you rise in the morning. Or they dictate that you get out and move your body a few times per week.

Over the past few years, neuroscientists have found that neural pathways are built into the brain around repetitive actions and behaviours. What's more, the more we repeat a behaviour and use these neural pathways, the stronger these pathways become.

Our habits are literally ingrained into our biology. But the good news is that your brain is not fixed due to its neuroplasticity we discussed. It can adapt, rewire itself, and change.

At the heart of this, our brains are designed to be keenly observant of what pleases us and what brings us pain or discomfort. Dopamine is released during pleasurable activities. This can range from sex to smelling freshly roasted coffee.

To understand just how powerful this neurochemical is, we need only look back at the early scientific work on it. For most of history, we can find philosophers and scientists questioning why people do things that are not in their long-term interests. They seek immediate pleasure while sacrificing longer-term security or safety.

In the late 1950s, there was a breakthrough in understanding. The researcher and pharmacologist Arvid

Carlsson would, in 1957, discover the neurotransmitter dopamine. Eventually, his ongoing work in this area would earn him a Nobel prize in the year 2000.

However, the initial reaction to his discovery was remarkably underwhelming. Few took much notice of it. The day's focus remained more on traditional neurotransmitters – noradrenaline, serotonin, and acetylcholine.[70]

Dopamine, however, would not stay out of the limelight for long. Soon, as the general understanding of brain physiology increased, the crucial role of dopamine became more apparent. It is not an understatement to suggest that the discovery of dopamine was a pivotal moment in modern neuroscience.

Since then, research has continued, highlighting that this neurotransmitter plays vital roles in everything from our mood, our behaviours, cognition, addiction, learning, and habit formation.

This is where we start to see where our habits come from at a biological level. The brain, which is always looking for patterns between behaviours and rewards, gives us a hit of dopamine when things go well. It's the brain's reward chemical.

The more we repeat an action, the stronger the neuro connection becomes, forming a habit. In turn, as Dr. Joe Z. Tsien, co-director of the Brain and Behaviour Institute at Georgia Health Sciences University put it, 'Habits, for better or worse, basically define who we are'.[71]

While our conscious decision-making is conducted in the prefrontal cortex, pattern recognition and habit formation are done in the basal ganglia – a region of the brain tucked away well out of sight of our conscious thoughts.

As we're not consciously aware of the activities in this region of the brain, it's perhaps one of the reasons why we find it so hard to break habits.

Of course, in the old world, in the less complex pre-industrial landscape, habits were lifesaving structures. Typically, they didn't need to change all that much over time. Why? There was little change happening in the world.

Our habits, therefore, led us to seek food and shelter, and avoid dangers.

Today things are different. The world has flipped. Now survival is about adapting to change, not clinging to the status quo.

Making decisions to change is also about breaking habits and routines. We have to get rid of doing things in a way that we know and find comfort in. In turn, we must replace this with an experience that is foreign, uncertain, and new.

In the early 2000s, I had the opportunity to spend time in various parts of the world as a youth athlete representing my county on the Alpine Ski Team.

One such place it took me was North America and the Killington Ski Academy: a place where both schoolwork and ski training could co-exist in a kind of utopia. During my time there, I met psychologist Dr. Jim Taylor who, among other things, was working on performance psychology, personal growth, and overcoming setbacks – three key areas any athlete at any level wishes to master.

In a recent article by Dr. Jim Taylor, he tackles what he refers to as the Law of Human Inertia. This he defines as 'The tendency of people, having once established a life trajectory, to continue in that course, unless acted on by a greater force'.[72]

It takes clear inspiration from Sir Isaac Newton's Law of Inertia. *A body at rest tends to remain at rest. A body in motion tends to stay in motion. Bodies will continue in their current state, whether at rest or in motion, unless acted on by a greater outside force.*

Bring this idea to the changes in the world around us and our observations of people's behaviour. What do they do? Do they change willingly, or wait until change is forced upon them?

This book is about getting better at seeing change, but that's of little use if inertia prevents action.

The point is, we have to be more open to change and more adaptable.

As we've just outlined, the problem with becoming more adaptable is that it's about breaking habits and making extensive changes to our life. Both bring more uncertainty to our lives and take us away from the status quo that we know and love. It's also super energy-intensive – therefore, we perceive it as hard.

The point this chapter makes is that transitions are painful periods in time. Sometimes our cognitive inertia has a role to play in this. We lag behind the ongoing changes in the economy. Our skills become outdated, perhaps irrelevant.

The trap comes in two forms; firstly, we don't notice the change until it is full-blown, and secondly, we gain comfort in not changing, because society doesn't appear to be either. Safety in numbers, right? Unfortunately not.

Change moves on regardless, and is typically accompanied by mass unemployment, financial crashes, and economic recession as money and people have to move from one side of the economy – the old economy – to the new one.

Few humans are flexible enough to simply jump to the new paradigm without significant external pressure. For most people, their way of working, their understanding of the world, and even their investments and finances are rooted in the old economy, and the 'old way'.

Such transitions don't just affect individuals and companies; they can also have effects at the global level. Countries' position in the global order change depending on how far behind or ahead of the new paradigm they find themselves at a national level.

The example we have already seen of this was in the third wave of innovation that centred itself around steel, electricity, and heavy engineering technologies.

As you may recall, Britain had led the way and been the trailblazer of innovation in this and the first two waves. This had earned them the position of global superpower, unrivalled by their peers. But by the time we arrived at the third wave, others were catching up – and more importantly, Britain was falling behind. Germany and the

USA were becoming the dominant engineering and steel players of the day.

Ultimately, Britain's ability to maintain its status as the number one global power faded. Tensions at the global level arose, just as I suggest they do at the societal level. Waves change everything.

As Britain's economic power faded, societal and geopolitical tensions rose, eventually resulting in World War I and World War II. Germany's defeat led to the US's newfound role as the world's hyperpower: the operator of the global free-trade economic order that we see being tested once more today in situations such as the China-US trade wars, and Russia's re-testing of western strength.

Chapter 9

Looking to the Future

∞

There are periods when innovation is more incremental. At these times, the changes we see around us progress and continue the same path: making improvements and tweaks.

In contrast, there are times when innovation jumps, and new technologies bring with them a new way of doing, starting a whole unique paradigm with it.

The largest progressions in humanity are the ones that take us on a new path – that see progress and time quite literally jump forward. These are also the most disruptive periods – new industries open and old ones fade. New skills are required and sometimes we need to unlearn what we thought to be 'true'.

The issue is we don't typically expect these jumps. We don't perceive or anticipate them. Partly because they occur so infrequently – once every fifty years or so.

As such, they stand in contrast with our everyday understanding and 'experience' of the world. They are quite literally different from the norm.

Our familiarity with incremental change leads us to expect only incremental change in the future, too. So, this is how we forecast the future, assuming that it continues pretty much as it has recently.

In 2007, researchers Sean Campbell and Steven Sharpe created a working paper as part of a Finance and Economic Discussion Series for the US Federal Reserve. In it, they took a long, hard look at the effects *anchoring bias* was having on forecasts in stock markets.[73]

What was surprising was the prevalence at which researchers found this occurring. Anchoring bias is our natural tendency to favour the first bit of information we learn about a topic. We subconsciously use this information to evaluate everything else, and any information we subsequently learn.

Campbell and Sharpe's findings suggested an extremely high correlation between the forecasts that professional forecasters were making and the previous month's results. In other words, they anchored their future vision on recent data.

This also corresponds with what we know about a bias called the recency effect (also sometimes referred to as 'recallability bias'). Essentially, we place far more weight on more recent data than we do on historical data points. We ignore the past and base our view of the future on today's situation.

We know little about why the recency effect occurs, but it does perhaps give us some insight into how memory works, and the effect of *active memory* and *short-term memory*. In this sense, recency bias forms part of the 'serial position effect' discovered by psychologist Hermann Ebbinghaus in his experiments looking at how accurately people could recall information depending on where, or the order, it occurred in a list.[74]

For us, taking into account the effects of anchoring and recency bias, the world we see around us is, on most days, not one of radical change. We can be 'change blind', not noticing how the world is changing because it looks and feels the same daily.

We witness few experiences of rapid breakthroughs; they occur infrequently. Therefore, they are unfamiliar and more likely to be considered 'one-offs' rather than something to expect in the future.

We also miss these periods of change because when they occur, there is no official neon-warning sign that lights up to tell us. The changes can remain unspoken by society for years. This is not to say they have no effect; they just lie below the level of everyday noise and out of sight, like strong currents and rip tides in the ocean.

As human beings, we are notoriously bad at seeing this kind of change. We are more attuned to noticing changes that occur quickly, like the dart of an animal out the corner of our eye that could spell impending danger. Many experiments have demonstrated that we are fundamentally flawed at seeing changes we do not anticipate or expect. Our perceptual screen tends to prefer conformity, i.e., it wants to see things today as they were yesterday.[75]

It's also the case that our understanding of the world is insufficient at these points in time. We cannot easily explain the new things we see occur if they are outside of our known world. Our understanding and sometimes even our vocabulary needs to update before we can understand what's happening. The truths we hold must update.

How truth becomes truth

The German Philosopher Arthur Schopenhauer in his 1819 book *The World as Will and Representation*, stated: 'Truth is only granted a short victory, between the two long periods during which it is either condemned as paradoxical, or disparaged as trivial'.[76]

A more modern version is found in the saying 'truth passes through three stages, first it is ridiculed, second it is violently opposed, thirdly it is accepted as self-evident'. This idea can be attributed to numerous authors and philosophers who have spent their lives looking at the process of how truth is accepted as such.

But just take a moment to think about this.

It's clear after the earlier chapters that this world we live in is a complex place. Because of this, we use narratives to help us make sense of the environments we're in.

We all have narratives for life; it's part of our desire for sense-making.

In turn, our narratives influence our worldview, which is another way of saying: 'This is the lens through which we observe the world'.

When we break it down, our worldview consists of the various aspects of our belief system. Our surroundings, background, environment, and emotions all affect our worldview. And, just like a camera lens, there are various filters through which we see the world.

This shapes our views and develops our understanding of the world. Therefore, having an awareness of what we believe, and what things we hold on to as part of our worldview, are essential prerequisites.

Once we have the awareness, we can observe things more objectively. But as said in the misattributed quote of Aristotle, 'It takes an educated mind to entertain a thought without accepting it'.

We often judge people and events according to our worldview without a second thought and according to the 'truths' we currently hold. We frame things according to our current understanding. We develop our principles, norms, and values according to our worldview. Add change blindness to the mix, and we fail to update these 'truths'.

All too often we let our community or society shape our worldview, and in turn us, along with the ideas we'll entertain or dismiss without much thinking.[77]

Curiosity is about being open-minded or at least entertaining a new idea that conflicts with your worldview, values, and beliefs.

Let's think about this in terms of trends and how these go from being nothing to mass adoption. Trends often follow an S-curve; initially, they are dismissed or not accepted, then there is slow acceptance, and finally, as the norms of society are changed, they mature and receive full acceptance. From here, the trend may slow down, or even decline.

It's the pattern of this, the S-curve, that you should pay attention to. The S-curve occurs in so many areas of life, from the adoption of new innovative technologies to our income earning ability throughout life, or the growth of population.

In a business setting, it goes something like this. Every business or product starts at the bottom of this S-curve. Its brand and products start out unknown, unfamiliar, and perhaps untrusted. As the product and business become more familiar and its credibility rises, so does its acceptance. Sales start to grow, trust grows, and market penetration rises. The growth may be slow initially but expands as consumers start warming to the product, then expanding rapidly as customers start shouting about this being *the best thing since sliced bread.* Eventually, growth tapers off again. This may be a new competitor coming into the market, consumer tastes changing, or completely new technology reducing its appeal.

Trends and the adoption of innovations do not move forward linearly either. For example, urbanization has been one of the most persistent trends over the past two hundred years – since the Industrial Revolution and arguably before.

According to United Nations research, the number of people living in urbanized areas has increased nearly five hundred per cent in just seventy years – rising from around 750 million to 4.2 billion. But the pace of the urbanisation trend is not constant. Just like other trends, its pace changes.

We also need to understand that trends don't continue forever. The same with each wave or technological paradigm; they grow, and then at some point, slow or even reverse.

The S-curve

The pace of change is a point we need to consider carefully. New emerging disruptive technologies can appear as if they have been lying dormant for many years – incorrectly labelled as technology 'that will never take off' or 'it's just a fad – people will come back to the good old ways eventually'.

The year was 1962 and Everett Rogers had just published his book *Diffusions of Innovations.* Everett's chief aim with the book was to describe the innovations' lifecycle and develop a framework or model that explained them.

His work is now widely adopted, particularly in the marketing world, being held as the go-to explanation when talking about the speed of new things being taken up and adopted.

While his book *Diffusion of Innovations* doesn't mention the adoption of consumer goods specifically, he made the point persuasively and universally enough that the terminology he introduced stuck and has become commonplace today.

We have Everett to thank for the commonplace phrases: innovators, early-adopters, the early majority, the late majority, and laggards to explain how people jump towards new technologies and products at different speeds.

In turn, we see how for new ideas and products to become mainstream, they usually have to go through a period wherein only a small fringe of society supports them. Sometimes for many years. But as the benefits of the technology become better known, talked about, and tested, more join the gathering and the adoption picks up pace.

Eventually, we get to the late majority and laggards who, for whatever reason, are the last to adopt the new technology and feel it is forced upon them in an instantaneous change.

The adopter-curve that Rogers suggested is more often referred to as the S-curve today, given its sigmoid shape. But the five stages, or adopter categories, are still at the heart of it.

As the adopter curve, or S-curve, became more widely discussed and implemented as a model of how ideas and products grow and become mass-market phenomena, others contributed to the work – not least in the book, *Crossing the Chasm* in 1991 by Geoffrey Moore.

As Moore put it in the book:

Every truly innovative high-tech product starts out as a fad – something with no known market value or purpose but with 'great properties' that generate a lot of enthusiasm within an 'in-crowd.' That's the early market. Then comes a period during which the rest of the world watches to see if anything can be made of this; that is the chasm. If in fact, something does come out of it – if a value proposition is discovered that can predictably be delivered to a targetable set of customers at a reasonable price – then a new mainstream market forms, typically with a rapidity that allows its initial leaders to become very, very successful. p. 7, *Crossing the Chasm*, Geoffery A Moore, 1991

Everett Rogers wasn't the first to suggest such growth patterns existed. An understanding of the S-curve started life some one hundred years before Rogers's work and can be found in the mathematical musings of the Frenchman Pierre-François Verhulst when he was working with data on population growth.

There are four basic types of growth curves: linear, log, exponential, and sigmoid.

The concept of the sigmoid curve is simple. There are two axis – let's say time runs along the horizontal axis, with performance along the vertical. What we notice in the S-curve is that there are two inflection points. The first is the start of rapid growth; the second is when that growth rate starts to tail off, giving an S-shape.

Of course, the vertical axis doesn't have to measure performance, this could be exchanged for nearly anything you want: sales, market share, or even what percentage of the population have adopted it.

The presence of S-curves in the world, particularly the world of trends and innovation, is astonishing.

While Verhulst applied it to ecology and Rodgers applied it to farming, Moore's work expanded the vision.

With hindsight, a quick glance back through history and we see that familiar S-shape in the adoption of many of the defining innovations of our era, from the telephone to electricity.

Using a percentage of the population as the measure, the angle at which these adoption curves are presented today is far steeper than those of decades gone by.

Take, for example, electricity, which was introduced and adopted by the 'early-adopters' as Rogers would describe. It took nearly twenty years before sixty per cent of the population adopted it, and a further thirty-five years before it was in virtually every home.

Contrast this with the colour TV and its innovation with roots in the 1960s. In just fifteen years, adoption was already closing in on eighty per cent of the population. That adoption curve is also seen in the computer, the mobile phone, the internet, and the microwave.

While there is little argument that change is speeding up, even the fastest innovations of today still work within a timeframe measured in years, not days or hours. They are still not the ultra-rapid type of change that is promoted through mass media.

The most common issue is we are already too preoccupied and overwhelmed to notice change occurring. We need to become far more observant.

The Kuhnian sense

Adding together some of the things we have discussed in the preceding chapters, most of us think far more in a Whiggish sense than a Kuhnian sense. What I mean by this is we believe that the issues of today will be gradually chipped away at until slow, patient progress overcomes them.

Whiggish, a term first coined in 1648, is a viewpoint that history follows a road of inevitable improvement and progression, which considers the past because of what is happening in the present.

A Kuhnian approach, however, says that science has no gradual movement towards reaching the truth. The scientific paradigm remains constant before a paradigm shift appears when someone proposes new theories because what is happening cannot be explained by current theories.[78]

Additionally, when a new 'radical' idea pops up, we are far more likely to be like the crowds that quaffed at Arrhenius whom we met in Chapter 3,[79] chanting, *please don't tell me you believe that stuff.*

Today the phrase 'paradigm shift' has, unfortunately, become so popular it's used to describe nearly anything that seems a little different. From the latest diet to a company that goes off-grid by sticking rows of solar panels on the roof.

But these things are rarely what Thomas Kuhn had in mind when he coined the phrase 'paradigm shift' in his book published in the 1960s, *The Structure of Scientific Revolutions.*

The central theory of the book, which remains in print today and is for its genre one of the bestselling books of all time, is that progress is not made linearly. In 1962, this was a pretty controversial view, and on top of that, who was Kuhn to even propose this? He wasn't part of the philosophical elite, but just a physicist.

The prevailing theory of the day was what we'll call the Whig theory.

As the great thinker Murray Rothbard put it, with Whig theory there was little need to read up on anything 'old' because progress is made in small steps that slowly and patiently build on the thoughts that preceded it.

Anything found to be incorrect is therefore automatically erased by the more modern works.

But Kuhn came along and upset this neat, orderly apple cart. Kuhn's assertion was that at key moments, thinking jumps forward through a set of normal and revolutionary phases.

During the periods of incremental innovation, progress is made in what looks like nice, orderly steps.

But during revolutionary phases, someone comes along and looks at a 'problem' that has been bothering society or hindering progress for some time and looks at it in a completely new light. At this moment, progress stops being linear but instead jumps. At these points, the way we see the world changes.

There are numerous examples, but to fit Kuhn's definition, they have to result in a fundamental shift in understanding or perspective.

Robert Anton Wilson, who was at various times in his life an American novelist, polymath, psychonaut, futurist, essayist, philosopher, libertarian, and self-described agnostic mystic, stated it quite succinctly when he said:

'Every fact of science was once damned. Every invention was considered impossible. Every discovery was a nervous shock to some orthodoxy. Every artistic innovation was denounced as fraud and folly. We would own no more, know no more, and be no more than the first apelike hominids if it were not for the rebellious, the recalcitrant, and the intransigent' (Robert Anton Wilson, n.d.).

Numerous paradigm shifts are already in the cards today. Including a move towards the *Age of Awareness*, the green energy transition, blended virtual and physical worlds, nanotechnology, and personalised medicine.

Change aversion is important to remember at these times –as Max Planck put it: 'A new scientific truth does not triumph by convincing its opponents and making them see the light, but rather because its opponents eventually die and a new generation grows up that is familiar with it'.[80]

Chapter 10

Information Revolutions

∞

The majority of our focus so far has been on the period since the Industrial Revolution. And with good reason. This is where we can most clearly see the waves of innovation – and arguably where they start, with the advent of harnessing fossil fuels to aid labour.

But there is merit in going back a bit further to the start of the Early Modern period that commences around the turn of the fifteenth century.

Why?

Because this is where we notice a special kind of revolution – *an information revolution*.

Information revolutions are a special class of revolution. In addition to the familiar technological changes, they bring something else: an increase in collective thought, and a rapid rise of collective intelligence. Given this, these are important to understand – particularly as we stand at the start of the third.

Over the past thirty years we have been living through the information technology age.

While the internet arguably connected the world like never before, we are about to find the applications being built on this today will be the real change.

Changes to how we work are encouraging more collaboration across diverse groups of people, geographies, and skill sets. With this there is also a philosophical and moral change occurring.

We are becoming more and more inclusive. More women are in positions of authority, racial equality is making progress, and we are starting to understand that neurodiverse individuals also bring a wealth of valuable opinions.

Just as in the two previous information revolutions that occurred in the fifteenth and nineteenth centuries, we are today harnessing more people's views and perspectives.

This brings new experiences and knowledge to the table. A new way to see the world, and often a new philosophy and moral code. It can also bring something incredible: a collective intelligence.

If there is no other reason to be hopeful for the future – and I think we have several – then this should be the one you cling to.

The abilities and knowledge of the human race have significantly levelled up at these key points in time as we have broadened the information pool and listened to a wide range of people.

Each of us has a unique experience of life, harnessing this collective experience and, in turn, intelligence that will propel the world forward in amazing and radical ways. This is far more than the simple number ticking of diversity campaigns.

Globalisation One: Age of Discovery

Dias & Columbus

The globalisation of the world started in the last fifteen years of the fifteenth century. Sure, there were periods before this where contact between different countries and people had been made, but changes during this time systematically changed how the world felt after the advent of European exploration in the 1400s.

One of the key drivers of this change was not just the display of heroic adventure by the likes of Bartolomeu Dias, the Portuguese explorer who became the first European sailor to navigate around the Cape of Good Hope successfully, and with it opened navigation routes from Europe to Asia. It was the advancing technology of the ships that they were sailing.

During the period often referred to as the Renaissance, several crucial developments aided the ability to navigate the world by sea. Among these were a growing knowledge of cartography, navigation, and perhaps the most important of all, ship building.

The most used ship for long-distance navigation at the start of the century was the *carrack*. A three to four mast ocean-going ship characterised by its deep and broad design. Some of the larger carracks would have reached a length of up to around forty-five to fifty meters. These ships also became the precursor to the large gallon ships that were used as cargo carrying vessels and warships.

But it was the much lighter and quicker *caravel* ships developed by the Spanish and Portuguese that made for the best exploration ships of the day. One of the key benefits of this design was their ability to sail into far shallower waters and sail upwind.

Bartolomeu Dias used two caravels and a larger support ship in his expedition round the Cape of Good Hope – or as he named it, the Cape of Storms.

While knowledge was increasing, Dias took a risk, just as Columbus would a few years later. Portuguese sailors had been exploring the African coast for decades, but they kept getting pushed back by the forces of the sea. Rumours would arise that there were sea monsters that could swallow ships whole.

There was also the issue of the Cape itself. If you made it around the Cape, would you even make it back? This was a genuine fear of the day. The combination of winds, tides, currents, and the clashing of two oceans makes the Cape of Good Hope a formidable sailing route even today. But we have to also factor in that at this time in the fifteenth century, little was known about what even lay beyond that point. It couldn't be seen by eye, so one had to question what would be encountered even if you could navigate a ship past that point.

At the time, Africa and its gold supplies were making Portugal rich, with some of the early expeditions along the African coastline coming back with both gold and slaves. Suddenly the cost of these missions was paying back – and handsomely, too. But passing the Cape of

Good Hope was still an unbreeched point. Soon, with gold flowing in, much bigger plans started to form, and the goal to sail around the Cape directly to Indian waters was hatched.

Portugal, whose power and wealth had grown, was already in trade with India for their spices. But without a direct sailing route, this was time-consuming and extremely costly as they had to complete large parts of it by land.

After many failed attempts and much-growing speculation that the Cape simply could not be navigated by ship, Dias was eventually sent to try. Dias took a new approach. Among his considerations was the Cape's proximity to the equator, and that there may well be 'westerlies'; prevailing winds that travel from the west to the east, just like they'd seen, and had knowledge of occurring, in the North Atlantic.

With this thought in his head, Dias decided to press on. It paid off. After four weeks of sailing through uncharted seas, he'd finally rounded the Cape.

While Dias made it round the Cape, and set the route, he would not be the one that continued to India. Dias wanted to press on, but his men refused. They'd seen enough and gotten far further than many of them had probably expected. There was still the fear of not getting back around the Cape, too.

A few years later, Vasco da Gama would take on the challenge, following Dias's route and pressing on to India to open up the trade route.

At the same time, Christopher Columbus was also hatching his own plans. Using the carvel ships to set sail from Palos de La Frontera in Spain, and knowing that the earth was round, his mission was to see if he could reach India by heading west. While his plan was sound in one regard, it failed on another point – the world was far bigger than he'd thought, and there were two continents between him and his goal.

What he instead discovered was the 'new world'. He made landfall in the Bahamas and named the locals he found there 'Indians'.

The ability to navigate the globe by sea was a turning point in history. The first full circumnavigation would occur a few years later in 1522, when just a handful of survivors who had set off under the command of Ferdinand Magellan some three years earlier would return to the Spanish port. Only twenty-two of the original two hundred and eighty sailors made it: Magellan himself died almost eighteen months before the voyage would end. But they had done it. They had managed to sail west and complete the very first circumnavigation of the world.

The term 'The Global Village', was coined by Marshall McLuhan, an author and media-theorist who captures the effects certain technologies can have on society when they bring people and knowledge together. In his book *The Gutenberg Galaxy: The Making of Typographic Man*, written in 1962, McLuhan argues that mass communication allows for a village-like mindset where ideas can be understood, shared, communicated, and transferred.

The age of discovery was a huge first step forward in this but was insufficient to bring about neither the first age of globalisation or the first information revolution by itself; for that to happen, it had to be combined with another technology that would facilitate the sharing and recording of knowledge.

As Jared Diamond put it in T*en Thousand Years of Solitude*, 'Inventions don't just get adopted once and forever; they have to be constantly practiced and transmitted, or useful techniques may be forgotten'. The accomplishments of the likes of Dias, Columbus, Vasco da Gama, and Magellan would form the delivery mechanism, but the printed word was that medium of storing and transmitting ideas that had been lacking in previous centuries.

Gutenberg press

Today the city of Mainz is a popular tourist destination in Germany. It's an ideal base to discover the region's wines and marvel at the city's famous medieval squares and half-timbered houses.

It's a beautiful place but is also one that we must not overlook in our understanding of the roots of our information-rich society today. Turn the clock back nearly six hundred years, and Mainz was home to one of the most important inventions of all time: the Gutenberg press.

Born around 1398, Johann Gutenberg held many positions throughout his life. A merchant, a blacksmith, and as the records also tell us, a goldsmith. At one point, he also appeared to be in financial difficulty when a business venture selling holy mirrors went south.

But it is perhaps the invention that carries his name that he is best known for even today – the Gutenberg press – and how this relatively simple machine, inspired by the region's wine presses he'd seen around him, would transform how information was passed from person to person, as well as from generation to generation. It was not just the intergenerational aspect of passing data from one to another. The press brought with it significantly lower costs.

Prior to Gutenberg's press, only those that could afford to employ a team of scribes to write out each manuscript by hand would have a hope of being able to 'publish' a title in the modern sense. The time it would take to complete a book by hand would depend on the size of the book, but, taking an example like the Bible, historian Martyn Lyons suggests it would have taken over a year to complete. That's an expensive project, and so it was naturally limited to a select few families that had the means to do so.

Gutenberg's press opened up the publishing market. With it came a keen and eager population to tell their stories, thoughts, and philosophical ideas that had, due to cost, been suppressed until now.

This story of the press is not simply a history lesson, but rather an allegory of sorts. Today we have gone through a new version of the Gutenberg press.

The internet and social media, together with key inventions such as the smartphone, have lowered the cost of publishing once more. Today the cost of publishing a blog, a tweet, or a webpage is very close to zero. Depending on the research, the speed at which the amount of all known information doubles is somewhere between two years and thirteen months. And it's expected, like Moore's law, to keep increasing from here.

The effect this flow of information has on society should not be underestimated. It changes things over time in significant ways. It changes us, too.

It's no exaggeration to place Gutenberg's press at the heart of many forces behind movements including the Renaissance, the Reformation, and the Enlightenment periods.

Knowledge is power, or more accurately, 'knowledge itself is power', as Sir Francis Bacon put it in the sixteenth century.

Bacon was right. Never has this statement held more truth as it does in the age in which we live today – where many, if not most, hold data and information as the most prized commodity.

Before Gutenberg's press we could number books in Europe in their thousands. Getting an accurate picture of just how quickly the number of books grew following Gutenberg's press is not easy. Estimates vary considerably.

That said, a good indication is that in just the fifty years following its launch, the number of printing presses in operation grew to around a thousand – each capable of printing around 250 sheets an hour. In other words, a single hour's production with the press could replace the annual output of a scribe.

It was not only Germany that saw the uptake in this new industry either; Italy also joined the printing race, along with Switzerland, France, Spain, and England by the turn of the century, as seen in the number of booksellers in cities.

At the time, the pace of information was like nothing seen before. The few thousand or so titles pre-Gutenberg's press were soon dwarfed by the sheer volume coming down the line, to the point that many of the largest cities such as Cologne, Rome, Venice, Paris, and London housed impressive bookshops and became something of centres of diffusion. Spreading with the books was not only new data to read but also the abstract ideas that came with them, which would revolutionize the way people understood life.

The press, and the books that flowed from it, would change the way people thought, inspiring a new era of learning and a new philosophy for society: individualism.

While for most, this was a good thing, it's worth noting that the changes in society were broad. Particularly for those that had up until this point enjoyed the position of 'controlling the information' and, if we take Sir Francis Bacon's view, this was the same as 'controlling the power'. The Catholic church was one such organization that saw its authority significantly undermined.

Globalisation Two: Age of Steel, Electricity and Heavy Engineering

Carlota Perez, who we met earlier in this book, has been a fundamental force in researching and understanding surges of technological development over the past fifty years. But let's remind ourselves of the attributes each wave has.

In one of her 1985 papers, she observed that each technology surge was characterised by the following attributes.

The new key technology of the age brings with it decreased costs, is almost unlimited in supply, heralds countless new opportunities for innovation, and forms a core part of society's methods of production and business.

When we find that the technology in question is also focused on speeding up and reducing the cost of 'communication' and knowledge transfer, we also get rapid globalisation and an increasing move towards Marshall McLuhan's *Global Village.*

Gutenberg's invention of moveable type led to a new wave of information which in turn fuelled the Renaissance, the Reformation, and the Enlightenment periods

We find this a common theme in information revolutions.

While the first of these information revolutions occurred in the combined achievements of global navigation and the Gutenberg press in the fifteenth century, we find that the second major move forward in globalisation from the perspective of information came in the age of steel, electricity, and heavy engineering.

The second phase of globalisation and information revolution would come around the 1870s with the telephone being invented, and the advent of voice transmission across distance instantaneously for the first time.[81] But it was also a time of increased global travel; for many Americans, trips to Europe became a normal part of life between 1890 and the outbreak of the First World War.[82]

Before the invention of the steamship in the nineteenth century, sailing routes, as we saw through the heroics of Diaz, Columbus, and Vasco da Gama, were controlled and shaped by the winds. The steamship changed this. The winds were also shaping something else – trade patterns.

The advent of the steamship was a pivotal moment for shipping and the world. New routes could be opened, and sailing times reduced considerably. In some instances, the travel time was cut in half.

The transition from sail to steam was also assisted by a secondary force – the US Civil War, and its subsidising of transatlantic mail. Steamships were faster than sail ships and could also complete the journey with fairly reliable and consistent travel times.[83]

By the late nineteenth century, the ships traversing the North Atlantic were some of the largest engineering projects on the planet. Crowds would gather at the ports to see off and welcome these gigantic ships as they came and went.

Fares trended down thanks to new ships that incorporated new engines, reducing fuel consumption significantly, and ships being designed to carry far more freight and passengers.

Once again, the world was getting smaller.

Increased levels of global travel and voice communication grew the levels of information flow and idea exchange. Just as we'd seen with the first information revolution, there was a corresponding rise in understanding during the second information revolution. In fact, the period this led to is often referred to as the Golden Age of Science, arising after the Second World War.

Of course, it would be far too big of a leap to suggest that the Golden Age of Science was entirely down to an increase in global information and a rise in the collective experience.

But we can say that as more perspectives were taken into account and listened to, the world changed.

Coinciding with these technological changes we also see philosophical changes contributing to the period of change.

America had emerged from the civil war that ended in 1865, and the move towards freeing slaves was established in the 13th Amendment of the US Constitution.

Each time we have an information revolution, there appears – at least so far – to be a far larger shakeup of philosophy within society. Cultural norms are challenged when information is democratised.

Globalisation Three: The Age of Information

The changing of both awareness and the philosophy of an age appears to coincide with advancements in the level and ease of information diffusion. This is something that we take particular note of today, given the information technology that surrounds us, and the increasing levels of information generation and sharing.

As with the previous two information revolutions, the speed and ability to deliver information has once again surged forward. Collaboration on projects now occurs over distances that would have made it impossible decades ago.

As we saw with the advent of voice communication through the invention and roll out of the telephone and intercontinental communication, today's video calls, email, and internet step it up once again.

There is one stark difference this time around. While the cost of sharing information was reduced in the first information revolution with the Gutenberg press, and again with telephone and shipping in the second, the level of cost reductions this time is significant. To the point that sharing information around the world is, in most instances, nearly free.

The cost of information sharing is always a key consideration. Before the first information revolution, only those wealthy enough to hire a team of scribes to work on 'publishing' a book could do so. The thoughts of those with less than this required level of wealth – which was most people – could not get their voices, messages, or experience heard outside of their small group of colleagues and friends, and at most, their village.

Many people have suggested that the level of globalisation has peaked. Reverse globalisation is the topic of the day, with many economists citing companies actively seeking to shorten supply chains that span the world and bring production and manufacturing back on shore with the aid of robotics, machine learning, and additive technologies. While this might be true in the physical economy, the most valuable commodity – information – is not following the same trend.

Globalisation is not going in reverse in this sphere – merely in the manufacturing world that belongs to past eras of change. I am, of course, not suggesting that we do not need manufacturing. We definitely do. Just as agriculture is needed today to supply us with food, its share of the global GDP has significantly and steadily declined. Today we produce food cheaper and from an economic standpoint this is far less significant.

The same will likely come true of physical goods. Take the rise of the circular economy, and the sharing economy that consists of far more efficient use of physical goods. Visit most cities today and you will be presented with sharable transport solutions – from pedal bikes to electric scooters. As our awareness of resource use continues to rise we also see the models of ownership changing – with the millennials and Generation Z-ers driving it.

While there is still much to figure out in the move toward the sharing economy, it is going through a rapid phase of trial and error – testing a multitude of models, particularly in the urban mobility category.

The globalisation of information is different. This is not going through a de-globalisation. In fact, it is increasing. The sharing economy on this front incorporates a host of sites that allow for the rise of the freelance world: WeWork, Upwork, Fiverr, and PeoplePerHour, to name just a few.

Perhaps the most potent example of such globalisation of information and knowledge diffusion can be seen through the race to create a Covid-19 vaccine. The story of how medical researchers developed a vaccine so quickly without compromising safety is another incredible human success story. One that should provide optimism for the challenges we as a human race see ahead.

The novel coronavirus variant, which was later named SARS-CoV-2, the virus that brings about Covid-19, was only identified in the very last days of 2019. Almost a year on, Pfizer became the first vaccine to be granted authorisation in the US. The ability to create and produce a vaccine in just twelve months is one heck of a feat.

Vaccines are complex things to develop. Before Covid, the reasonable, expected time taken to create one would be around ten years – if a solution could be found. What changed this time?

Thousands of researchers around the world came together. The technologies they were using allowed them to collaborate in real time and incorporate new shared data. Just ten days after the virus was identified, researchers successfully mapped out its genetic sequence.

While this is a clear and ready example of the power that comes from our increased ability to collaborate, the roll-out of technologies coming down the road from the likes of the Metaverse will significantly turn the dial up. We are living in a time of rapid change.

In the not too distant future, there will be a point when the immersive experience of virtual worlds will be so powerful, captivating, and all-encompassing that it will seem just as 'real' as the world we inhabit now. True information sharing and globalisation of information, thoughts, and experience will occur at this point.

Chapter 11

The Age of Awareness

∞

The most recent wave of innovation, the information age, has transformed our world experience in numerous ways. As we explored in the previous chapter, it has brought a higher level of connectivity, information sharing, and the ability to collaborate at previously unimaginable levels. As these technologies progress, so will the human capacity to combine experience and knowledge, and our collective intelligence will rise with it.

This latest wave of innovation also brought with it a change in the production system, or era, that we're in. We are transitioning away from the production era, which started with the Industrial Revolution. In its place, we have now begun to move into the cyber-kinetic era.

While we have outlined these two changes in previous chapters, we need to think about an additional, and very significant, change that this most recent wave of innovation has caused – our ability to measure.

At the heart of the information technology wave is the ability to log, observe, and measure far more details about our surroundings and what's going on. The semiconductor is, in some sense, a chip that observes and responds to changes – be these signals of light, heat, or something else.

From this pursuit, the level of data and information has grown exponentially, and so have the methods and approaches to understanding it, decoding it, and assimilating it. New disciplines have popped up, and with them, phrases such as 'data mining' and 'big data'. These approaches set about trying to extract meaningful information from impossibly large databases.

Technology has enabled us to more accurately and more frequently capture what's going on. Today we can log, record, and measure almost anything at increasingly granular levels. Be this by using ultra-high-resolution cameras from satellites in space to track the movements of millions of harp seals displaced by the melting Arctic Sea ice, to our sleep patterns, heart rates, stress levels, and whether we are optimally oxygenated.

There can be downsides to this level of tracking – information overload and an increased tendency to focus on only an increasingly short time horizon. But there are benefits, too. We are becoming more aware of ourselves, the world, and others around us.

This awareness – something that I refer to as the Age of Awareness – is a direct result of our increased ability to measure. Without measurement, we would still be in the dark on many things we care so passionately about today. We are undergoing a change in cultural philosophy.

While it remains vital to be on the constant lookout for potential technologies that could be the next paradigm-shifting event, we also need to hone and develop our intuition. We need to capture the zeitgeist.

Beyond the innovation cycles

We have already considered some of the huge megatrends that hold an influence on innovation, and in turn what direction the world takes. But let's extend our vision.

Further out from the fifty- or sixty-year-long innovation cycles, we come across even longer periods of time. Eras or ages that have a common zeitgeist. Thinking on this timescale can yield us valuable insights: we can capture the general characteristics, motives, and ambitions of a certain period in time.

In this sense, the period from the Industrial Revolution in 1771 to the birth of the information age in the 1970s can be characterised under the archetype 'the age of industrialisation', and the period that preceded it, the 'age of sail'.

While this is in many ways a large oversimplification, and there is much more to these periods if we want to fully understand them, there is also a level of clarity that we attain when simplifying this far.

As we aim to get a 'feel' for the time, the trade-off seems, for the purpose of understanding long-term trends, an acceptable one. Of course, once we have gained a high-level overview, there is much benefit in diving deeper into the histories of each period to understand them at a more granular level.

Coming back to today, the age I suggest we're approaching is what I label 'The Age of Awareness'.

My reason for this is that in nearly every domain, we are turning away from mass production. In addition to this, our view of both human labour and natural resources is shifting away from simply seeing them as expendable inputs. In its place, the new growing culture is moving rapidly towards one based on a greater understanding of the natural systems and ecological balance. There is growing realisation that fellow humans are individuals rather than homogenous groups.

Companies are starting to see the real value of ensuring the boards and groups are made up of diverse groups of individuals, going beyond race and sex, to incorporate background and neurological makeup.

Environmental awareness is just the tip of the iceberg

It's hard to turn anywhere today without bumping into an environmental headline, campaign, or effort. And with good reason. Climate change, if the science is right, is perhaps the greatest challenge humanity has ever faced.

While climate change may take more of the headlines than its fair share, it would be a mistake to believe that this is the only area in which we are becoming more aware.

Our environmental awareness is just the tip of the iceberg. The Age of Awareness is far bigger than this. It is incorporated into nearly every aspect of life, from our health to the inequalities that we wish to resolve.

In 2012, the United Nations Conference on Sustainable Development was held in Rio de Janeiro. The aim of this particular meeting would be a significant one and one that would aptly capture the growing awareness of what's going on and what we want to put right.

How? Well, there was time set aside on the agenda to lay out a blueprint that would form a set of universal goals. These goals could then be used to assist with a more sustainable and positive path of future development. A framing of things to think about.

The set of Global Goals, as they would be called, would cover a number of high-ticket item areas that you would expect to see. Climate action became Goal 13. Life below water and life on land respectively became Goals 14 and 15.

Also included in the 17 Sustainable Development Goals were areas such as good health and well-being, decent work and economic growth, and peace, justice, and strong institutions.

While each goal has its own targeted sphere of influence, it is when we step back and take note of what they all collectively signify, that is, a single aim: a world with far greater awareness and responsibility for our actions toward others and the natural environment that we inhabit.

The growing health and wellness sector

In 2010, a number of reports came out showing that while consumers stated that they wanted ethical, authentic, and sustainable products, their shopping habits said otherwise.

They were still purchasing based on cost alone. What was even stranger was there was a widening gap emerging between their stated desires and their behaviour.

With customers only verbally stating they wanted 'better', companies were slightly reluctant to change what they produced.

But in the past few years, shopping habits have seen a noticeable shift. Awareness is growing and becoming something far more than just a surface-level attitude or stated desire.

Consumers today are asking tougher questions of companies – even shunning those that do not live up to their claims. Of course, this isn't universal. Not everyone is aligned with this view, but a growing segment of the population is. And as we know, this is how trends develop. Slowly at first, but the rate of adoption then increases more and more rapidly.

It's perhaps most interesting to ask: why now? Why are these things changing today?

When we dig a little deeper, we find a few key forces at work. The first comes from the repercussions of the Great Financial Crisis that began in 2008. Millennials (those born between 1981 and 1996), particularly the younger end of this group, were just entering the workforce at the time the recession hit, as well as the oldest members of the generation behind them: Generation Z (born since 1997).

Their early working lives were more financially restricted than previous generations. They had to learn to live with less, spend less, and do more with less. Using the concept developed by demographers William Strauss and Neil Howe, through their Generational Theory, the Great Financial Crisis was an *age location in history*. A significant event that affected an entire generation.

As the recession passed, this behaviour didn't. Gen Z-ers' spending habits and approaches to life are vital for us to understand. As with any new generation, they bring a pervasive influence on the global economy and the societies and relationships around them.

In one study run by Cassandra, the business intelligence agency, they suggested that Gen Z-ers would not only become a significant consumer in 2020 but also that their spending behaviours were influencing older generations. The Gen Z-ers' view of the world was rubbing off on their parents.

On the surface, it appears that this Gen Z generation is far more brand aware than previous generations. It's clear that they're happy to spend their money on such items. But there is a subtle change that we should notice here too. They are purchasing brands that help them reflect who they are as individuals to the world. Their shopping habits and their personal identities are far more closely linked than in previous generations and times.

Over the coming years, this new group of consumers, with unique views on spending habits, will make up around forty per cent of global consumption.[84] With their preference for more ethical choices, combined with this spending power, it will likely have a meaningful impact on how companies operate.

In a survey conducted by the global consulting firm McKinsey, they found that seventy per cent of Gen Z-ers say that they try and buy products from companies that display ethical considerations. Some eighty per cent can recall at least one corporate controversy, and over half try to find out more about how the product is made and its origins before they purchase.[85]

To think that this started in the recession, or even with Gen Z, would be short-sighted. One of the key lessons of this book is to 'look for the long tails of change'. Things do not simply happen overnight; instead, seeds are sometimes sown decades before the visible change takes place.

If we want to better understand the world and how it works and changes, we must get better at being more aware of these changes. We must be more observant and curious about change.

Gen Z-ers might be the generation that brings the Age of Awareness to the main stage, but it's a movement with its origins firmly rooted in the 1970s.

To illustrate this, let's take a look at the food and drink market. It is a market that I am familiar with, having started a craft distillery, Snowdonia Distillery, in 2015 with the early signs that there would be rising consumer demand for more authentic and better-quality spirits.

Within the food and drink sector, the 1950s and 1960s were a time when food lost its way, at least from a nutrition and quality point of view, with the rise of canned food. It is little surprise that as quality fell, some started to re-advocate for real food. Freshly cooked meals and thinking more about where the food you were eating was coming from. Books such as *The Whole Earth Cook Book* came out in the early 1970s. One outlet for this was the start of the organic movement in food, which just a couple of decades before had been derided and ridiculed by consumers and farmers alike.

By the time we get to the 1990s, we start to see that this increase in consumer demand for organic foods pushed new regulations in the food industry to define organic standards. The organic movement was just the start. Since then, we have seen a return of small local craft breweries that have increased the quality of beers, after a long period when mass production took away the flavour of beer in search of cheaper products.

Consumer knowledge over this time also increased. Most people have a far better understanding of the nutritional requirements of their body and how best to nourish it. Whether people follow their own advice or not is another topic.

We have seen the authenticity movement of food and drink continue to grow. The countless rise of craft distilleries worldwide is a testament to this movement – people are seeking higher quality, better produced, and ethically produced goods.

These trends change consumption and production patterns. It's estimated that over six per cent of Generation Z-ers follow a vegan diet: and with this, it is little surprise to see the rise of meat substitutes and plant-based meat companies such as Beyond Meat come to the fore.

According to research by the Good Food Institute, the sales of plant-based meats have grown twenty-seven per cent in 2021 and stood at an estimated total sale value of over $7 billion. That's expected to keep growing too, with the cost of such products coming down and becoming more accessible.

But it's not just food and climate change we see driving the Age of Awareness. Health and wellness spending is up with Gen Z as the driving force and often described as the 'ultimate wellness consumer'. As such, wellness is being redefined as people desire to not simply 'keep healthy', but also optimise their human condition – considering everything from the correct nutrition to tips on *Biohacking Your Brain*, which is the latest title from neuroscientist Dr. Kristen Willeumier.

Gen Z-ers are far more aware of the health risks associated with fast foods, stress, high sugar diets, and are even warier about medicines. But they also have a better handle on optimising rest, taking key supplements, and monitoring their sleep hours very carefully.

From service to experience to uniqueness

The ability to monitor, record, and analyse data does not only affect how we see the world or the things we buy. Over the past couple of decades, it has also affected the businesses themselves and how they provide and market their goods and services.

Traditionally, businesses followed rigid service-based models that took little in the way of consumer feedback into account. How a consumer felt on an emotional level was not a necessary input. Products were produced and services rendered. The consumer, to most businesses, was a homogenous class of people.

But over the past few years, businesses have had to transition away from this service-based model to an experiential model. A model that does not have one-way lines of communication flowing from the business to the consumer, but instead has two-way chatter.

In other words, businesses have had to move from a transactional model, being paid for a basic level of service, to an experience-based model, where the views and feelings of the customer are taken into account. It is rare for business to remain both ahead of the competition and at the forefront of their sector today while operating purely on the old service-based model. The emotional needs of the consumer have to be catered for.

It's not that businesses didn't care about their customers in the past. But rather, with the assistance of technology, and the attitudinal change of consumers not wanting to be seen as a homogeneous group, the customers' opinions and views became far more valuable. Even essential. Businesses that do this well show their customers that they care and are authentic and real.

The system has moved from a one-way service system to a circular experiential system. On the back of this, we can see the growth in numerous rating sites. These sites show prospective clients and customers what to expect – even ranking a hotel or restaurant on how it might suit couples, business travellers, or families.

The next generation are shaking this up again. The move afoot this time extends to the personalisation companies will be asked to supply their customers. Not just engaging in communication – but understanding and tailoring services to their customers unique needs.

Just as the move from service to experience required greater feedback between the parties, and a circular flow of information, the move to uniqueness is part of the growing Age of Awareness. This next step requires businesses to have an even deeper understanding of their customers' needs, preferences, and tastes – expecting their journey with the business to be tailored.

Gone are the days when the paying customers were mere 'consumers' of service and information. It's a subtle but powerful shift. It is not just the 'service' industry that this affects. The 'age of personalisation' as it is sometimes referred to, challenges all business models, from professional services to retail businesses.

With the advances in technology, we have more data at our fingertips than ever before. As discussed, this is both a blessing and a curse. But in the age of personalisation and uniqueness, it's a technology that has to be leveraged.

Grocery stores track shopping behaviour and tailor discounts and reward schemes to an individual's shopping habits. This contrasts starkly with previous times when reward schemes were one-size-fits-all. The only filter was the very generic idea that your shop attracted a certain type of consumer, and therefore on average, they would want 'X'.

Marketing has changed, too. Years ago, large billboards would convey a single message in a scattergun approach, hoping that from the thousands of people that walked past, it would make a connection with a small but profitable group.

The focus has changed direction, from the business to the consumer.

Marketing and ads are now directly targeted through nearly all mediums, phones, apps, internet browsing, and even the personalised TV ads you see.

From vertical to horizontal management

Change can be seen with in the structure of businesses, too. During the mass production era, human input on the whole was seen as little more than a quantifiable amount of labour: a man, woman, or child who could watch over, shovel, or re-stock a machine so that production wouldn't slow.

That has changed. During the information age, there were the early signs of a move that started to increasingly value the human attribute of workers: their ideas, creativity, and innovation.

Businesses, at least the more successful ones, understand that their employees are far more than simply labour-producing droids. If managed and treated correctly, they bring creativity, ideas, and innovations that otherwise are lost.

In other words, we are becoming more aware of the *human nature* of humans. Perhaps the most visible aspect of this change is the move from the old vertical management structure – where strategic planning and idea generation was reserved for those only at the top – towards a horizontal management structure that allows each employee far more freedom, independence, and voice.

The Age of Awareness appears to be gathering momentum whichever way you look. From our awareness of food, exercise, and health, to the structure and service of businesses.

Section Two

The Inside View

In this section, our focus will turn more inward. We will start to look at the positive effects of optimism as a coping strategy – even if the incredible story of human ingenuity, innovation, and adaptability has failed to inspire you. We will also explore why adopting this mindset can even lead to a more accurate picture of the world.

We also need to consider the effects of the mass media and information overload, which is commonplace today, before diving into how the structure of the way we consume information can affect our understanding and views.

Finally, although biases are seen as the negative outcomes of mental shortcuts, they can also be helpful. We will end this section by thinking about the times and ways we can use some of these mental shortcuts and pattern recognition to build a far better intuitive understanding of what's going on.

Chapter 12

Replacing Pessimism

∞

There have been many core themes in this book so far. The one that inspired the writing of this book was the observation that times of uncertainty, which naturally occur with periods of rapid change, also bring about a rise in anxiety, fear, and pessimism. Linked to this is also the decrease in creativity.

As humans, we find it far easier to visualise what has been over what might be.

The past is more tangible.

The future is more abstract.

But the most inspiring story that we will ever hear is the one of how humanity, against all odds, overcame impossible hurdles. I suggest that the future will be no different.

Today, looking out to the future, we certainly have hurdles to overcome. If the past is anything to go by – and I suggest it is – then we should adopt a somewhat optimistic stance.

When we combine our human history with the Age of Awareness and the third information revolution that we are going through, the accomplishments of the past will likely pale in comparison to the innovation of what lies ahead. With this, it propels us towards the next golden age – a smarter green economy, based on paradigm-shifting technology that makes our current world look primitive. Just as we did with previous eras and civilisations.

Unfortunately, this is not the account that most people carry around in their heads. Instead, they hold a pessimistic view – something that goes hand in hand with periods of significant change and turbulence. The more uncertain the environment, the more anxious and fearful we typically become. Through evolution, *fight and flight* has today become *anger and fear*.

The world is perhaps the perfect environment for stress, allostatic overload, and those undesirable neurobiological responses to chronic uncertainty that we looked at back in Chapter 4.

One key point consistently comes across from conversations with people on this topic over the years. We have become so short-term in our thinking that we seem to forget this incredible, awe-inspiring story of human achievement.

Throughout this book, I continually repeat the need for us to take a step back and see this big picture. In fact, I don't think we can look forward without first looking back.

While I hope to instil a far higher level of general optimism in your vision of the future by increasing your awareness of innovation and how it works – how it jumps forward, and how it has transformed societies in the past – in this section, we turn inward. We start thinking about change from a cognitive perspective and get better at seeing it.

Our starting point in this chapter is why you might want to adopt a more optimistic mindset, even if you can't, at first, see the incredible signs of positive world-changing innovation going on around you.

Don't get me wrong; this is not some 'rainbows and unicorns' chapter. I am not going to suggest that if you think happy thoughts hard enough, all our issues magically disappear. Not at all. Instead, there are numerous benefits to having an optimistic mindset during times of massive change. For one, when we're optimistic, we become far more resilient to change, more creative, and more collaborative.

This is kind of in line with Tuchy's Law: *worry is like a rocking chair – it gets you nowhere.*

In recent decades, psychologists have focused on this positive and optimistic mindset. Specifically, they have focused on its significant relationship with physical and mental health, persistence, motivation, career success, satisfaction, and resilience.

Psychologists define optimism as a positive attribute characterised by the expectation that good things will happen.[86] It is the belief that the future will be favourable, even when things are challenging.[87]

In general, optimism, as a component of emotional intelligence, allows us to acquire, master, and use it in different aspects of our life.

But why does this matter? Well, one thing is for sure, if we are to overcome the issues, obstacles, and threats up ahead, then we will need to collaborate as a human race. We will need to come together, harnessing our collective intelligence. These things rest on us being more tolerant, open-minded, and welcoming of new ideas. They rest on us being optimistic.

"Future is your optimism"

Martin Seligman, an American psychologist who has studied the theories of positive psychology, divides happiness into three domains: 'The past is your feelings of well-being, it is the life story you tell yourself. Present is what is usually called happiness, it is how you are feeling right now. And [the] future is your optimism.'[88]

People with a positive mindset focus on the good side of a situation and learn from the lessons implied. The belief in a better future is founded on a clear purpose. Yet, optimism is not only about happiness and positivity; it is also an 'explanatory style' at the core of how we explain the causes of situations.[89][90]

Simon Sinek, a British-American author and speaker, explains this in a straightforward manner: 'Positivity is blind. Optimism is the undying belief that the future is bright, but it is not a denial of the current state'.[91] Hence, optimists trust themselves because they know they are prepared to face any situation and make things happen on good terms.

They take constructive steps to solve their problems rather than giving up. If something good happens, optimists think of what they did to obtain such a result, but if something bad occurs, they treat setbacks and frustrations as temporary.

Optimistic expectancies are linked with superior performance on complex tasks. A natural optimist knows that problems and obstacles do not prevent personal growth or progress. On the contrary, they understand that bad things are a necessary part of life; therefore, they cope with stressful situations more successfully than pessimists.

Morgan Housel points out, 'Optimism is not about being the best at what you do; it is about never being forced to quit doing what you do'.[92] Optimists know that they can survive day-to-day obstacles by learning what hard work produces over time. They look for meaning in adversity, which makes them more resilient.

You probably know the story of Edison. At least his pivotal role in developing motion pictures, the light bulb, and electrical power. But many have suggested that his real skill was his ability to endure setbacks. When tragedy bested him, he did not crumble – but, rather, lurched forward.

In the early evening of 10 December 1914, Edison's lab, which housed countless records, notes, inventions, prototypes, and experiments, burnt to the ground. At the age of 67, most would have expected this to be the end of his career. His life works lost. But not for Edison; while his work was still ablaze, he supposedly said *I'll start over again tomorrow*.

Both optimism and hope are mindsets rooted in the belief that positive future outcomes are possible.[93][94]

The bright side of optimism

There is countless research that studies the connection between mind and body.

It has been scientifically demonstrated that if our emotions change, our brain also does. Our thoughts even intervene in the functioning of our immune system. Optimism is often associated with concepts such as confidence, coping, growth, functioning, and goal achievement.[95][96] There is also evidence of the positive correlations between this attribute and psychological well-being.

Anticipation, a key factor of optimism, is a powerful predictor of psychological well-being. The latter consist of six elements: self-acceptance, purpose in life, autonomy, personal growth, environmental mastery, and positive relations with others.[97]

Optimistic people experience a higher quality of life compared to pessimists. So, the benefits of being optimistic are abundant. It has also been demonstrated that when the principles of positive psychology are applied to human performance, people lead happier and more efficient lives.

Since motivation and action are the results of what we believe, optimism can protect us against uncertainty and despair. This is certainly something needed in a rapidly changing world, which at times can appear unfamiliar. Indeed, there is a substantial relationship between positive attributes and self-assessed anxiety[98] because the balance among feelings such as sadness, angst, anger, and depression are all associated with people's degree of positivity.

Positive feelings also encourage creative problem-solving and improve interpersonal relationships. In the case of optimism, it gives us the openness to change, inspires the uninspired, and helps us maintain the hope that we can improve our circumstances.

The adaptive value of optimism

We often encounter significant transitions throughout life, such as attending school or university, moving, getting a job, starting a relationship, having children, or retiring. Each phase introduces us to new information and experiences to which we must adapt. Optimism is again crucial to surviving these transitions thanks to its 'adaptive value'.[99]

Optimism is adaptive because it encourages efforts to cope and achieve. As optimists expect positive outcomes, they continue to exert effort to reduce, eliminate, or manage stress, indicating that they are more likely to overcome challenges and effectively regulate emotions.

For example, several studies highlight the benefits of holding an optimistic mindset during high school. They show that optimism plays a vital role in adapting to new educational environments. It affects levels of general interest in academic studies. Students with high levels of self-reported optimism adjusted better to school and experienced less stress.[100][101]

These results align with other studies that demonstrate positive connections between optimism and resilience in university students.[102] Scholars showed that higher levels of optimism upon entering college are also associated with lower levels of psychological distress. Optimistic students are in fact, less depressed, less anxious, and feel more supported than students with lower optimism.

Consequently, optimism gives us the strength to continue adapting to change. It allows us to keep our goals alive and be motivated to achieve them. We can also maintain expectations for success and positive reactions to adversity, change, and emotional demands.

Optimism is healthy

Another way in which optimism significantly influences us is through the promotion of a healthy lifestyle. It is also associated with physical well-being and fewer depressive symptoms.[103] Current research indicates that it might also mitigate health matters, e.g., improvements in the incidence of infectious diseases or chronic illnesses, mental illness, or access to life-saving innovations.

Optimism builds barriers against the impact of physical stress and health problems.[104] Optimistic people have better pain management, improved immune and cardiovascular function, and greater physical functioning. Additionally, some scholars suggest that higher levels of optimism may be an essential psychosocial resource linked to reduced risk of premature mortality.[105]

Optimism and cooperation

Optimism can enhance performance in career development, business management, and sports leadership. It can set the common ground for better cooperation with less conflict, uniting divergent groups with the hope and conviction that they will achieve beneficial outcomes.

McAfee et al.[106] emphasised that in an era of significant changes like we live today, 'optimism could help unite people to act.' Its 'infectious nature' creates an atmosphere of confidence and gratitude that motivates people to work together. In this sense, a positive mood can predict greater negotiation skills, critical thinking, and the willingness to reach an agreement and compromise on group decisions.

When used in practice, positive psychology enhances team coordination and problem-solving. Within a workplace, positivity, hope, and emotional resilience strengthen performance by making positive change. An optimistic atmosphere around a communal task motivates individuals to cooperate and invest in the solutions.

In the same way, a positive mindset opens the door to creativity, curiosity, and the design of strategic responses because optimism broadens the attention scope. Moreover, these aspects lay the groundwork for innovation, which increases our productivity and helps us discover new opportunities. In the professional field, optimism takes us where we need to be, developing the necessary knowledge to achieve our goals.

Authors such as Alexandra Terrill also describe optimism within the social context as a behavioural preference for active engagement in personal interactions.[107] Consequently, optimists also promote positive feedback, facilitating interpersonal functioning and social support. For example, in romantic relationships, optimists and their partners enjoy greater relationship satisfaction and mutual support.

The benefits mentioned above allow optimists to maintain an emotional advantage over pessimists. This advantage is derived from emotion-focused coping and can compensate for losses in the effectiveness of problem-focused strategies. Because of this, most scholars agree that a growth mindset breeds success. It is clear that optimism is highly beneficial, but can it be learnt?

Learnt optimism as a strategy to take advantage of reality

Optimism generally comes from our nature, as some of us were born with an optimistic temperament. Researchers also suggest that in some cases, a positive mindset is influenced by childhood experiences. Even so, optimism is also determined by our life experiences. The good news is that we can learn how to be optimistic. Like helplessness and pessimism, optimism can be situation-specific and acquired through experience.

We have already discussed how positive thinking often involves believing that all will be fine (in the absence of evidence, or even in the face of contrary evidence).

However, the negative ideas that follow adversity are usually inaccurate. A learnt optimistic mindset is more about accuracy and taking advantage of reality.

The concept of 'learnt optimism' – proposed by Seligman[108] – suggests that there are no limits to the advantages of more positive inner dialogue, and encouraging thoughts can be cultivated while negative self-talk can be challenged. It promotes the courage, mindfulness, introspection, productivity, and persistence necessary to face challenging or overwhelming tasks.

Countering negative thinking is at the core of learnt optimism. It is how you cope with negative statements and is characterized by the cognitive duality of sustainable hope linked to a realistic appraisal of obstacles. Eventually, it can create a means for stress to become tolerable and even empowering.

On the other hand, the cultivation of learnt optimism is based on the awareness of who we are and what we want to be. Hence, we find that our optimism grows from viewing our strengths and seeing problems as external to ourselves. It is from here that we form more positive future outlooks.

Each person or circumstance is subject to change and has a potential for growth, no matter how challenging or traumatic a problem is. Learnt optimism suggests there is a future to consider and that tomorrow holds hope for transformation. Nevertheless, optimism also has a dark side that we must be aware of.

Excessive optimism can be harmful

Believe it or not, optimism is not always beneficial; as the old proverb says, 'too much of anything is bad'. The first reason is that excessive optimism could reduce your sense of urgency, causing you to fail to protect yourself against threats. For instance, excessive optimism can lead people to overestimate their ability to cope with hard times and, in certain situations, even ignore a threat until it is too late.

Secondly, the excessive optimist's worldview and mood departs from reality, making them more vulnerable to the consequences of a traumatic experience than the pessimist.[109]

Psychologists encourage people to avoid what is called 'optimism bias' – the tendency to overestimate the likelihood of positive outcomes and downplay the possibility of negative ones.[110] All the benefits of optimism that we've listed above can be diminished when someone strays too far or becomes excessive in their optimism, and can lead to failure to develop problem-solving skills, as well as high expectations that are impossible for anyone to fulfil.

Such cognitive and motivational distortion leads to fantasy, affecting people's expectations of personal life events in favour of their beliefs. They believe that the probability of encountering negative events is nil. Overall, 'blind optimists' see life through rose-coloured glasses, unable to cope with uncertainty or disappointment.[111] Therefore, expecting unrealistic results may increase their dissatisfaction.

How could this happen? The optimistic bias results from different factors such as lack of information, poor awareness of one's cognitive skills, and the defence of one's self-esteem.

How much is too much?

To avoid optimism bias and finding ourselves in the excessive optimist camp, our optimism must be rooted in accepting the possibility of negative outcomes.

In other words, our optimistic viewpoint to take chances and pursue challenges should have a dose of truth or realism about the risks involved in every situation. This is one of the best ways to build resilience and achieve goals.

As a final thought, optimism is a mental attitude that goes beyond ignoring problems; it is a different approach to analysing our experiences and taking constructive actions. A high level of optimism can improve physical and mental health and help us maintain positive feelings that combat pessimism and fear – two things that can rise in times of change.

Optimists reset their sights on their changed realities and significant transitions, coping with daily frustrations and making the best of the situations they are facing.

We must avoid falling into unrealistic optimism. Optimism leads to better health and greater success, but only when it goes hand in hand with a realistic worldview. In today's world, such a mindset has become more critical than ever to navigate change, increase self-management, and build resilience.

Along with curiosity, I fundamentally believe it is the key to the human race elevating itself to the next golden age.

Chapter 13

Information Overload

∞

Hansgrohe Group, based in Germany, is one of a few truly international players in the sanatory industry. Founded in 1901 by Hans Grohe, they quickly grew a reputation for creativity and quality, based on a creative culture that still exists today. It was, therefore, little surprise to see a firm like this take a not-so-typical approach to their research. Sure, there was tons of research into the products they were producing – but that's not the research we want to discuss.

In 2015, they commissioned Scott Barry Kaufman, Ph.D., who specialises in cognitive psychology to look into the question of just why people seem to have their best thoughts in the shower.

Kaufman sank himself into the task, surveying over four thousand people aged between 18 and 64 from eight different geographical markets that Hansgrohe Group had a presence in around the world. The results spoke for themselves. Seventy-two per cent of people have personally experienced having new ideas when in the shower. Interestingly enough there was even data to suggest, particularly among the younger cohort, that some of them were intentionally taking showers just to see if they could juice out any fresh insights and ideas.

But why? And what relevance does this have for us in considering the trends, megatrends, and transitions around us?

Kaufman's research concluded that the shower is a near miracle of a place. It is an oasis for the stressed-out, modern mind. A place of calm where we can actually get to the end of a thought.

As Kaufman put it, 'The calm, solitary and non-judgmental shower environment may afford creative thinking by allowing the mind to wander freely and may cause people to be more open to their inner stream of consciousness and daydreams'.

This makes a lot of sense when many theories of creativity rest on the idea that previous ideas and experiences are given space to collide and come together.

Einstein called this *combinational play.*

Let's be honest for a moment. Our modern world isn't exactly the ideal environment for combinational play. It's way too noisy. We are way too distracted. Our attention is fought for over hundreds, if not thousands of times a day. If we think of the marketing industry as an industry employed to grab your attention, then the amount of money spent on getting your attention is staggering. In 2021, it was projected to reach over 52 billion USD.[112] That's up 276 per cent over the last five years alone.

Of course, it's not just marketing that grabs our attention. Today the modern world is filled to the brim with content, blogs, vlogs, podcasts, films, box sets, docu-series, whitepapers, and breaking news. Most of it is at our fingertips, and much of it is free whenever we want it – and even sometimes when we don't.

The way most of us live out our day is far more suited to a condition and state of overload and overwork: the exact opposite of Kaufman's shower-oasis.

Let's backpedal for a moment. Has it always been like this?

While it's easy to think that information overload, a term often spoken about today, is a phenomenon unique to our time, we'd be mistaken. We'd be right that it's getting worse and far more commonplace – but it's certainly not new.

Before the information age, it was far more common in the upper classes, who, with a little extra money (sometimes a lot of extra money), could buy more information than the working classes. Today, information inequality has been largely removed – information is accessible to nearly anyone whether they want it or not. That's mostly a good thing. But we need to learn how to cope with such a torrent of information at our disposal.

One of the first researchers to describe information overload was Georg Simmel in 1950. He noticed that there appeared to be a sort of overstimulation of residents of cities and linked it with an inability of these residents to react appropriately to novel stimuli.[113]

In his presentation 'Designing organizations for an information-rich world', H. Simon (1971) defined the problem of information overload as 'a wealth of information [which] creates a poverty of attention and a need to allocate that attention efficiently among the overabundance of information sources that might consume it'.[114]

The exponential increase in information exposure ever since has been noted by many researchers. At the heart of this increase is the advent of computing, leading to expressions of information overload, which began to be described in the 90s by Shenk[115] as 'data smog' and by Oppenheim[116] as 'information fatigue syndrome'.[117]

Even in the era preceding the advent of smartphones and mass-consumer mobile internet, information overload has negatively affected information consumers.

As technology becomes increasingly automated, rather than reducing the burden on information workers, it has instead created a demand for more information to be processed faster.[118]

With the advent of information technology, reports and data which would otherwise take days or weeks to be processed, can be processed in seconds.[119] Despite the calculation improvements, the human decision-maker's cognitive capacity remains limited.[120]

As the time between calculations decreases, so does the decision-maker's opportunity to reflect and contemplate their data.

Fibre optic: the demand for fast data

Our demand for faster, cheaper information flows has not shown any signs of slowing. In the late 1950s, we hit a physical wall.

A limit to just how fast we could transfer information. For those who wanted more information and wanted it quickly, that presented an issue.

We struggled to significantly increase data transfer speeds using the existing copper wires.

While many had been playing around with glass rods, the level of light scattering and subsequent loss of signal strength caused many issues when trying to transmit data over any realistic distance, say, between cities or even countries.

Progress was slow. But as we've seen through this book, innovation is not always linear or developing at a constant pace. Hurdles and problems, rather than acting as eternal barriers, often act like a coiling spring from which innovation leaps forward, just like a tightly coiled spring when finally set free.

As we reached the 1960s, that metaphorical spring of data transfer speeds was nearly ready to make the leap. There was a breakthrough in the technology surrounding it. Charles Keun Kao, better known to most simply as Dr. Kao, born in Shanghai in 1933, moved to England to complete his education, and eventually gain his Ph.D. in Electrical engineering from the University of London.

Kao overcame a critical issue that would pave the way for the fibre optic internet we commonly use today.

Before Kao's work, most people felt that using glass rods to transmit information wasn't going to work. But this didn't deter Dr. Kao.

Based on his years of experience, he had an intuitive feeling that the issues of signal strength and light scattering could be overcome. And with that, to Dr Kao at least, this project was not dead, but far from it.

Kao's approach was to purify the glass being used to the point that more brilliant white light could pass through it, and the light scattering issue could be overcome.

Just as with the Gutenberg press, while it would take time for the new technology to find buyers and users, the new technology and the speed at which information could be passed was an opportunity people couldn't pass by.

The US Government was one of the first to install fibre optic technology at the North American Aerospace Defence Command (NORAD) centre at Cheyenne Mountain.

Its public debut would come in the race between AT&T and GTE, both laying down fibre optic cable between office blocks to try and become the first working system. While AT&T's cable could carry more information, GTE managed to win this first optic race.

Soon after, larger projects, such as the Boston-New York-Washington corridor, were completed.

It wasn't long before the increased speed of data transfer and, specifically, the reduced lag in time found its way into one of the most time-sensitive business sectors – the investment community.

Just as Sir Francis Bacon had acknowledged that information was power, to the investment community, knowledge, especially the type that others don't have yet, was real power – even if you only have it for a fraction of a second over your competitors.

Latency describes the time it takes for the signal to travel from the point of origin, in this example say the time between the New York Stock exchange and the receiver, wherever that might be.

Flash trading, as depicted in Michael Lewis's book *Flash Boys*, is about reducing this lag as much as possible. It's one of the reasons that high-frequency traders and proprietary traders are often found clambering for locations as close to the exchange as possible, because even in a world where the speed of information can travel at close to the speed of light along fibre cables, it's still only the speed of light, and therefore distance still matters.

The shorter the distance, the shorter the time to recover an information packet and send a response.

Even at the speed of light, the distance between the East and West coast of America has a noticeable impact.

Gaining price information fractions of a second before the rest of the investment market brings a natural edge.

If you're running the right software and your computer is fast enough, it brings an opportunity to buy and sell again at a profit before others have even seen the price change.

Uncertainty and decision fatigue

As the Covid-19 outbreak became a pandemic, the investment markets, which I spend my days analysing and watching, went into free fall.

Uncertainty over the future outlook of the entire economy was called into question – and for good reason. Never before had the world co-ordinated a near-total shutdown of the economy – even if this was only to be a short, temporary measure to 'flatten the curve' as it was first put across.

Investment markets are fruitful places for us to look when we want to see the effects of sentiment, uncertainty, and information overload.

Organisations such as the American Association of Individual Investors have maintained a weekly sentiment survey since 1987. To compile this, they ask members, who are typically professional investors, a simple question. What's their outlook for the stock market over the next six months?

As we came into the middle of March 2020, the data came in from the surveyed members – those holding a negative outlook for the next six months had climbed by fifty per cent.[121]

This was not surprising; it only took twenty-two trading days for America's leading stock index, the S&P 500, to fall thirty percent from its record high on 19 February 2020. That represented the fastest thirty per cent sell-off EVER in history, a record set back in 1934.

But this wasn't just an American phenomenon. In almost perfect synchronisation, the world was locking down.

Pew Research Centre released their research on the unfolding situation on 1 April 2020, wherein they tried to assess how many countries were imposing lockdown restrictions.

Their findings were, as the headline read, 'more than nine-in-ten people worldwide live in countries with travel restriction amid Covid-19'.[122]

Market volatility spiked to historic levels, yet another indication of fear, stress, and extreme uncertainty among investors.

During this time, and with the almost constantly changing situation in various countries where we held assets, my working hours extended. I was glued to the news and any real-time indicators I could find.

From Google's mobility trends, which shows data on how many of us are visiting shops, restaurants, parks, or even staying at home, to the data on the number of flights landing and taking off and the prices of petrol at gas stations; I devoured it all.

The near-constant news cycles of evolving restrictions, lockdowns, and rules on which businesses could or couldn't operate in various regions had me glued to the news. A change in a country's approach to restrictions could significantly impact on the price of assets.

I started to feel grateful for the end of trading in the US on a Friday, and the much-needed fleeting rest that would be granted until markets reopened in Asia on Monday morning.

I am sure you will have your examples of this time.

But if you have ever been grateful just to reach the end of a day because of mental exhaustion, then you know the feeling.

In these situations, recalling information that would normally be on the tip of your tongue becomes harder.

You struggle to make simple decisions and hold conversations. While we usually describe this as being tired or even exhausted, psychologist Roy F. Baumeister coined the term 'decision fatigue' to explain this situation.

Your brain becomes overloaded and not only does the quality of your decisions around the 'stressful' thing decrease, the quality of decisions across all domains goes down with it.

It doesn't only occur at the end of a long day either. In situations where everything seems to be going wrong, and just you can't seem to find a solution – you'll experience decision fatigue then too.

It may help to think of decision-making as much like a battery that has a certain amount of energy to give but is ultimately a finite resource. The more decisions you make, the more drain on the battery until eventually there is no charge left, and making any decision seems virtually impossible until the battery is again recharged.

Decision fatigue is also referred to as ego depletion. It's still an emerging concept, so there's still a lot we don't know about it – some even dismiss it as a theory. But just watch people who have had a stressful day and have to make more than their 'normal' quota of decisions. You'll notice something common among them – they seem to have lost a certain amount of willpower.

This makes sense when we consider that much of our understanding about decision fatigue is based on the Strength Model of Self-Control.[123]

In this theory, humans have limited decision resources at their disposal. It's like a muscle that fatigues after exertion.

The experiments run by researchers Baumeister, Bratslavsky, Muraven, and Tice in 1998 looked at four different environments of choice, active response, and self-regulation – suggesting that if they could increase the amount of effort people had to use to complete a task, they should subsequently see a depletion of a person's decision-making ability because of 'drawing on a common inner resource'.

In one of the experiments, they got participants to eat radishes instead of the good-looking great-tasting chocolates they put in front of them.

This seemingly annoying but perhaps benign task had profound effects on each individual's subsequent problem-solving abilities. They had been using up their inner reserves of self-control, and now there was less in the tank.

In another experiment, the researchers got their participants to suppress emotions to see what effect this had. Once again, the energy expended on controlling thoughts harmed future cognitive problem-solving abilities.

Since Baumeister's 1998 experiment, ego depletion has been one of the core and important phenomena in social psychology. Over three hundred subsequent studies have looked to replicate this early work.

In 2011, Shai Danziger, Jonathan Levav, and Liora Avnaim-Pesso published their paper. What the trio of researchers asked was an intriguing question.

If decision-making was a resource-depleting task that affects our ability to make subsequently taxing decisions, then this should show up in society. Regularly.

A year before, Jonathan Levav, a professor at Columbia University, had been looking at the cost of thinking in regard to purchasing decisions. Specifically, he focused his attention on the order that options were presented to consumers and how this affected their decision-making.

He put together an experiment focusing on the myriad of options people face when buying a car.

First, he split the consumers into two groups that would be exposed to 144 options when building and configuring their new car. However, one group would be presented with the more complex questions at the start of the process, while the other group would first tackle the easier questions that had fewer options to consider.

The more often a consumer simply went with a default, Levav suggested, that might signal fatigue.

Just going with it because 'it' was the easiest option. He found that those who were presented with more complex options first had a much harder time as the process went on – tiring far earlier than the group that started with the easy questions.

Levav wanted to look at this in more detail.

Of specific interest was why people were accepting the default once cognitively drained.

To Levav, the judicial system seemed to be the place that might hold the answers. Here was a system and processes that based its decisions solely on the facts that were known and a check of these against the best understanding of the law.

There was no room for simply taking the 'default' option – or was there?

The results that came from this experiment were shocking. Findings support once again that as a judge uses up their cognitive reserves, their decision-making changes too, with the most favourable rulings made either first thing in the morning, or after a break when cognitive resources have been sufficiently replenished.

But what about at the other end of the session when the judge has already had to make repeated rulings? The researchers found that just as with the German car buyers, as the cognitive load took its toll, the default – the easy option – was more often than not taken: 'show[ing] an increased tendency to rule in favour of the status quo'.

This does not just apply to significant life-changing decisions, purchasing big ticket items, or for that matter, building our scenarios for the stock market.

We all have countless choices to make each day; in fact, some of the research suggests that on average, we make around thirty-five thousand decisions every single day. As rapid change confronts us, this also increases cognitive load. There are not always easy answers and as we looked at before, it's mentally taxing when we enter a hypervigilant state.

Covid-19 might present us with the perfect example of how our mindset and cognition are affected when there is a rapid transition from a familiar environment to one we find foreign.

There was a detectable change in the general population and how they were feeling. Tasks that used to be easy – like answering your child's question, figuring out what's for tea, or even putting away the laundry – suddenly started feeling far bigger and more taxing for a lot of people.

It wasn't just the social media posts that pointed to this.

A survey by the American Psychology Association revealed that while most Americans were coping pretty well with the lockdowns, changing rules and regulations around the pandemic were leading to a growing number who reported feeling overwhelmed with simple day-to-day tasks. The researchers behind the survey cited a number of catalysts, including the need for increased decision making, unfamiliar routines, and increased need for risk assessments in daily life.

But in these situations, we should be cautious of decision making. We cling far tighter to the status quo, or simply the default option. In turn, we become far more susceptible and open to suggestions, which is where we will go next – the environment of our decision making.

Chapter 14

Perceptions, Decisions, and Our Environment's Role

∞

In the early 1970s, two psychologists, Daniel Kahneman and Amos Tversky, started to look at how we make decisions from a more scientific and empirical perspective.

Of particular interest to these two researchers was how we make decisions under conditions of risk and uncertainty. What mechanisms allowed us to make a decision and what information was used to make it?

By the early 1980s, the newly created field of behavioural economics was born and quickly started demonstrating that we consistently make significant deviations from purely rational, logical decisions. The mental shortcuts we take and the cognitive biases that arise were at the heart of this.

We can think of cognitive biases as mental illusions or thoughts subconsciously influenced by external data and experience. We take these mental shortcuts with good reason: it saves our brains from having to work too hard.

The findings from this research made not only huge waves in psychology but also shook classical economic theory. Until this point, most traditional economic models held that humans made perfectly rational, well-measured judgements. Spoiler: we don't.

Over the years since these initial findings, Kahneman and Tversky's prospect theory has been built on, refined, and studied by hundreds of thousands of academics, students, and professionals worldwide.

Over time, the list of cognitive biases that have been 'uncovered' keeps growing nearly every year. But before we consider some of the biases that affect our worldview and perspective of the future, we need to consider the environment in which we take in information today.

Echo chambers

The sheer amount of information around us today leads to an increase in cognitive fatigue. Our brains take more shortcuts to counter this, which directly contributes to the biases in our thinking.

We are sense-making animals, fine-tuned to detect subtle patterns and changes in the environment around us. But the structure of the information we have around us today can throw us off course. We live in a world of *echo chambers* that can distort what we see and how we perceive things.

Echo chambers can be described as the tendency, specifically on social media, to find more of the stuff and people we like. As the saying goes, birds of a feather flock together.

In our digital worlds, we're increasingly surrounded by people with similar viewpoints of the world. This was especially noticeable before the last US general election when one compared the Republican and Democratic camps.

Over the past few years, there has been some intervention by social media firms to counter this phenomenon, but it's not easy. There are many connections, and we love finding others who agree with us. This force is so magnetic that even the strongest interventions and algorithms have a tough time preventing the development of divergent networks.

This also leads to a sort of Pygmalion Theory. One where the world as we would like to see it eventually appears to materialise. Why? Simply because of the sheer number of people joining and rallying around a particular world viewpoint.[124]

It must be said that not everyone agrees that the echo chamber exists.

A paper produced by Seth Flaxman and others at Oxford University examined the browsing habits of fifty thousand US social media users. What he found stood in opposition to an echo chamber theory. Instead, he concluded that social media users escaped the echo chamber by being exposed to opposing viewpoints. The 2016 University of Ottawa study reached a similar conclusion.

Flaxman commented: 'It seems counterintuitive, but direct browsing often just consists of one or two sites that you regularly read – such as the BBC and CNN – while by its nature, social media will expose you to a number of other sources, increasing the diversity'.[125]

These two studies aside, more recent research suggests that echo chambers are alive and well. In fact, it could well be one of the main draws of social media – we get to share, connect, and communicate with others who share our orientations and viewpoints. There is even a word for it: homophily.

This leads to the natural polarization of society into groups with opposing viewpoints, whether they also visit sites that hold opposing views or not.

The digital footprint we leave behind in our online activity provides researchers with large amounts of data to study polarization in different contexts. Be it the US presidential elections, radical groupings, or other political movements in various countries.

From this, it can be observed that political orientation has been a primary driver of separating societies into various opposing online groups. With users far more likely to receive information from peers sharing the same average leanings.[126]

Filter bubbles

Filter bubbles and echo chambers are similar, but there is an important distinction.

While echo chambers relate to who we connect with, filter bubbles are about algorithms that find more of the stuff we like.

In other words, our online behaviour sets off an algorithm sequence to tailor our feeds with content based on previous search history, likes, engagements, shopping habits, and comments.

In short, it means that the internet gives us what we want.

The issue is that filter bubbles isolate you. The term 'filter bubble' was first coined by internet activist Eli Pariser. When you're in a filter bubble, it means that the algorithms, in the way that they filter out what you can and cannot see, isolate you from opposing and important viewpoints. You will not know you are in a filter bubble because the algorithms don't ask for your permission or tell you that such a bubble is active. Therefore, avoiding them online is virtually impossible.

Pariser also calls a filter bubble a 'personal ecosystem of information'. It isolates us from a feeling of cognitive dissonance by screening or limiting what we see, i.e., by impacting our perceptual screen.

Why do you think certain ads pop up 'coincidentally' after searching for a similar product? With each click we make or comment we share, social platforms and search engines use that information to create targeted advertisements. As we continue to operate this way, these search engines refine their algorithms more and more until you seem to always have adverts for items you might be interested in popping up.[127]

Research conducted in 2018 highlighted the Google filter bubble manipulation of search results based on personal data. It came up with several findings.

Most participants in the study saw search results unique to them that could not be explained by time or location issues, to name but two variables.

On the first page of search results, Google showed various user links that were unique only to them and not to the other users in the study.

Although people searched at the same time, they were shown different results within the video and news info boxes.

First being logged out and then in again also did not change things. In short, it was almost impossible to maintain a level of privacy.[128]

So, Google was essentially controlling the content participants were able to see. Google is controlling the content YOU see.

Groupthink

Groupthink is a phenomenon that occurs in groups when the desire to ensure conformity and harmony is so great that it leads to dysfunctional decision-making. It typically results from the group either wanting to avoid conflict or make quick decisions instead of spending great amounts of time pouring over complex datasets. The result is that it leads to single-minded and blinkered decision-making. This often happens in homogeneous groups.[129]

The collapse of Swissair is an excellent example of groupthink that is often upheld in business schools. A short time before the airline's collapse, the number of directors on the board was reduced, resulting in certain areas of expertise being 'culled'. What was left was a number of directors, whether this was the intention or not, who all had similar backgrounds and shared the same standards and values. This resulted in a situation where, due to the pressure to conform and avoid conflict, the directors failed to question gross mismanagement and poor decisions, eventually leading to the airline's demise.

The smaller the specific area, be it a business or committee, the higher the risk of groupthink because the 'gene pool' is much smaller and tends towards homogeneity.[130]

Groupthink is often referred to as the Asch paradigm and it originates from an experiment conducted in 1951 by Solomon Asch at Swarthmore College, which laid the foundation for conformity studies. In this experiment, groups of eight male college students were given perceptual tasks without knowing that in each group, only one person was a student, and the rest were actors. Only the actors knew the true purpose of the experiment.

Each student received a card with three lines on: labelled A, B, and C, and a separate card with a single line on it.

The participants then had to say out loud which of A, B, or C the single line on the separate card correlated to in length.

The actor was told beforehand which response to give. A total of eighteen trials were done. In the first two trials, the actors and the subject gave the same answers – which was the correct response.

But for the remainder of the trials, the actors gave incorrect responses. Led by this answer from the actors, participants followed their lead. In his opinion, regarding the study results, Asch put it this way: 'That intelligent, well-meaning, young people are willing to call white, black is a matter of concern'.[131]

Our cognitive liberty is, therefore, circumvented or even directly undermined in various ways. No example of this is more to the point than the Cambridge Analytica scandal.

In the 2010s, Cambridge Analytica started to harvest data from as many as fifty million Facebook profiles based on their online preferences and behaviours, with the apparent aim of subconsciously targeting and influencing election results.

Although different in its scope, this scandal was nothing new. An experiment by Facebook targeted almost seven hundred thousand users whose newsfeeds were algorithmically altered to observe changes in their behaviours. This study showed the massive potential of social media to alter people's emotions on a large scale by making them happier or sad without their awareness.

Apart from the data privacy and protection implications emanating from the two case studies listed above, an arguably more important consideration is that the present online ecosystem that we all are part of daily presents a shortcut to the subconscious mind that can induce addictive behaviours, or at least layered or manipulated behaviour.

You do not have to be able to tap directly into people's brains to influence choices but simply mine the data they regularly use to be able to build up a profile of an individual's likes or dislikes and subtly change this.

As the online sphere of the world grows and becomes more immersive, we need to become far more aware of the structure of the information environment we're in.

Echo chambers and filter bubbles should be a big wake-up call for everyone who surfs the media regularly.

Social media has had a massive impact on the way that we consume information and news.

Ministry of Public Enlightenment and Propaganda

If we leave behind the natural evolution of filter bubbles and echo chambers and hunt for extreme examples of cognitive manipulation, the lessons only become more critical.

In times of war, it's common for nations to use some sort of propaganda. They employ campaigns that unite their citizens and rally the nation to rise in a shared narrative against a newfound 'enemy'.

During the Second World War, teams of artists were employed to design posters calling for troops in both Britain and America. These campaigns went far beyond marketing.

Today we see propaganda in the military parades from nations like North Korea, China, and Russia, which have dual roles of remembrance for those fallen as well as reminders of current military strength, both for their citizens and other nations that might be on-looking.

But when it comes to propaganda campaigns, few have done it as well as Hitler's Nazi Party.

Founded on 14 March 1933, Joseph Goebbels headed up the propaganda machine, the Reich Ministry of Public Enlightenment and Propaganda. This was a key strategic part of Hitler's wish to shape the worldview of the people of Germany, and vital to understanding the eventual persecution of the Jews.

The fact that the information to be dished out was neither truthful nor accurate mattered little to Hitler.

In his book *Mein Kampf*, he states that propaganda must '...be limited to a very few points and must harp on these in slogans until the last member of the public understands what you want him to understand by your slogan. As soon as you sacrifice this slogan and try to be many-sided, the effect will piddle away'.[132]

In saying this, Hitler demonstrated without question his knowledge of manipulation. Our worldview as humans isn't completely fixed. Our personality and our experiences play a large role, but crucially, Hitler knew it was also shaped by something else: the information we receive. Furthermore, when these things combine, they form the lens through which we perceive the world. In other words, our worldview is flexible. Even malleable.

Taking this one step further, all these variables influence what we perceive as right or wrong, or what is true.

It forms a sort of positive reinforcing feedback loop. How we perceive the world depends on our worldview, but our worldview depends on how we view things and how much importance we give to them.

Understanding this, Hitler and Goebbels developed a carefully balanced system that was slanted towards building an optimistic viewpoint of the Nazi government. At the same time, their message was designed to divide society into two opposing viewpoints as far as views of the Jews were concerned.

It would be another twenty years after World War II ended before George Gerbner would develop the most cited cultural theory, cultivation theory, which observed the media's influences on our worldview.

At its core was the claim that the amount of time we spend in front of the television or media affects our views and personality. What we view and watch encompasses our reality. Hitler's attempts did not stop at public broadcasting. He literally planned to change history.

An August 1940 directive from Keitel conveyed Hitler's order to Army High Command. It included several instructions, namely the destruction of certain memorials, and a systematic alteration of the country's institutional memory. Also included was the elimination of so-called hate monuments and inscription panels, and German weapons were to be displayed as war trophies at Zeughaus (military museum) in Berlin by 1 November 1940.

In his most powerful show of force and as an attempt to show up history, Hitler ensured that the French signed the armistice in the same railcar in Compiègne and at the exact location as in 1918. Afterwards, Hitler ordered the railcar to be taken to Berlin.

It is clear what Hitler wanted to do – he wanted to recast Germany as the ultimate victor of the Great War and the Allies as the losers.

Although Keitel's directive sheds new light on Hitler's plans for revising history, it goes further than that. It shows that one should carefully consider whose narratives we trust. When our perceptions are altered, it doesn't just affect how we view the past, but the future too.[134]

My experiment with newsfeeds

In 2016, I decided I would try something – an experiment of sorts. I would cut out most of the mass media and social media hype from my daily news intake. I wasn't entirely convinced about how it would go or even if it would work in practice for that matter. I had a business and my job as an investment strategist required me to know what was going on in the world.

At the time, I was completing my MSc research, which focused on how we make decisions in conditions of uncertainty and how information influences our evaluation process. It was clear the information you take in has a massive effect. But I was noticing something else. In the rush for mass media to be first-to-post, they were starting to exchange quality reporting for speed.

In today's world, where social media users are instantly on the scene of breaking news stories, media outlets have to try and keep up. I am not suggesting that all media is rubbish. It is essential to maintain freedom of speech.

If every breaking news site had to go through some kind of peer review process, it would simply be too slow.

The unexpected result of my media-cutting exercise wasn't detrimental. In fact, quite the opposite.

Today I see the world differently than it looked when I was unaware of my echo chamber and filter bubble. This book is, in part, a result of it.

The other change I made was to switch from sources of information that aimed to be the fastest to those that sought to be accurate and informative. I subscribed to monthly and quarterly periodicals and created multiple social media accounts that gave diverse filter bubbles.

I am not suggesting that you take such radical steps in your life. But I can tell you that when you make the move to cut out some of the hyper-paced stuff, if done correctly, you don't suddenly become uninformed. In fact, in my experience, the opposite happens. I've found that the most important news stories still get to me.

Another reason I went down this route was the realisation that there is a section of the mass media industry that is more aligned with *entertainment* rather than *truth*. Let me explain.

After cutting out the sensationalized hype of the breaking news cycle, something else happened. Something that surprised me – my outlook on the world and life became much more optimistic.

I'm not the only one that has found this. When researching this topic for this book, I came across an article by the author Mark Manson, written in the same vein. After realizing that ninety-nine per cent of the news he was being fed was pretty much irrelevant to the decisions he made in real life, he too cut it out. He also found that the pessimistic views he had started to lift.

Bringing this back to our views of life, watching bad news repeatedly tends to become a form of self-fulfilling prophecy. People start believing what they expect to see.

Ryan Holiday has a term for how news stories are written today: outrage porn.

'"Outrage porn," we call it, checks all the boxes of compelling content – it's high valence, it drives comments, it assuages the ego, projects guilt onto a scapegoat, and looks good in your Facebook Feed'.[133]

Holiday's observation cuts straight to the point. Much of today's breaking news is little more than clickbait, with the content aimed to spark an emotional feeling of outrage. It's a winning formula for the news industry – not only can you sensationalize the reporting of an event, but you also get a second article reporting just how much people found it 'outrageous'.

Psychology Today, the US-based magazine and online content creator, ran an article in late 2019 commenting on just how the media's habit of latching on to our hardwired bias for negative stories was rapidly distorting our view of the world:

'Watch, read, or listen to the news, and you're likely to come away believing that the world is rapidly descending into disaster and chaos'.[135]

'Last to breaking news' is perhaps a strange tagline for any news or media company today. I mean, who wants old news?

But it perfectly sums up the ambitions of one particular periodical, *Delayed Gratification*, a magazine dedicated to a slower pace of journalism, exchanging rapid-fire content for deep thinking. But why?

For many people, their only window into the world is through their own experiences and a reliance on the mass media outlets and the stories they post. It rests on the hope that news is accurate and includes the most important stories you need to know about. But mass media outlets survive through catchy headlines and being the first to breaking news.

They must be the first, because what use is a breaking news station that only tells you events hours after you already learnt about them from your social media network broadcasting live from the event?

Delayed Gratification took a different approach, asking, 'What use is a breaking-news station if the content isn't even worth reading?'

Speaking at a TEDx event in Madrid in 2014, Rob Orchard, the owner of The Slow Journalism Company, the company behind *Delayed Gratification*, spelled out just where media reporting had got to.

Within three minutes of Rob being on stage, he'd not only painted a picture of how breaking-news journalism had lost its way in the previous twenty years, but also gave the inside track on how breaking news sites, in their compulsion to be first to get the news out to the world, write multiple stories covering different potential outcomes of an important upcoming event. In the process, they cook up quotes and stories that never happened.

The example Rob gave that day was of the *Mail Online*'s reporting of the Amanda Knox story, originally convicted of murder in 2009 but freed on appeal in 2011.

Yet that's not what the *Mail Online* reported.

The reasons for this error vary. As Rob tells it, the journalist was sitting in the courthouse on the closing day of Amanda's appeal case and heard the word 'guilty' and assumed that Amanda had indeed lost the appeal, and that the murder conviction was upheld.

Others say it was a poor translation of the judge's verdict. Either way, it's not the reason *why* the error was made, but *what* the error highlighted. Which was that the *Mail Online*, in its ambition to be the first to post the story, had cooked up two potential articles depending on which way the verdict would go.

The one released had vivid descriptions of Amanda Knox beside herself, weeping uncontrollably as the verdict was given. There were stories of how the victim's family showed compassion and the feeling in the courthouse; but it was all fabricated. Believable, yes – but true? Not even close.

Chapter 15

The Biases in Our Thinking

∞

Let's return to the world of biases. We use a variety of mental shortcuts due to our brain's desire to make things easy. The complexity of the world forces us to simplify and focus on specific aspects of life.

We simply can't take everything in without overloading and burning out very quickly.

Take a straightforward example. You're looking to purchase a new phone and you have a basic list of requirements. Perhaps this would be things like memory or the camera's quality.

Even though your requirements are simple, and you know what you're looking for, you're likely to be confronted with a large range of options – models, manufacturers, and even retailers.

Of course, one option would be to take the time to thoroughly research and read up on every single handset and every single aspect, down to the technical differences between Apple's A13 chip and Huawei's Kirin 990 chip. But this would be a considerable and time-consuming task.

An alternative option (which most of us take) would be to pick the handset that appears to meet the essential criteria, plus has that slight edge over the others. Maybe it's a lower price or that it comes in a colour we love. Essentially, with this option, we've achieved our criteria and, as a bonus, we've saved a whole load of brain power. A job well done.

But we've decided without fully knowing if this was the absolute best choice possible.

This type of decision-making process is an example of what we'd call *satisficing*. The term was originally coined by Herbert Simon in 1956 to describe decisions that both *satisfy* and *suffice*. Most commonly, this happens when there is no apparent easy answer. Unsure that all the hard work involved in finding the absolutely-best-possible-option is worth the effort, we satisfice.

At the time of Simon's work there was growing interest in the decision-making process. Economics still held that individuals almost always make optimal decisions. And that we humans are very careful to make sure that our conclusions are rational and logical.

But this isn't how we make decisions in the real world, and completely rational choice behaviour is sporadic.

Instead, we tend to take shortcuts.

If this wasn't enough, our preferences aren't stable either. What we want today may not be what we want tomorrow. Our choices change depending on the situation we're in, too, and can be influenced by completely unconnected things – such as the weather (shown to influence our mood), stock prices, and how generously we tip.

Sunny weather makes us happy and puts us in a good mood, increasing optimism and sharing. Bad weather has the opposite effect.

Returning to the opening point, there's simply way too much information for us to process slowly and logically. So instead, we take mental shortcuts we call 'heuristics'.

While such heuristics can help us make fast decisions, it is also important to be aware of how these can lead to biases – skewed thinking. Especially when making a judgement call about what the future may look like.

In earlier chapters, we have already come across a number of biases that frequently crop up when thinking about the world around us.

But we also need to be aware of a couple more that are vitally important. Let's deal firstly with confirmation bias.

Confirmation bias

It's suggested that we humans have had a basic understanding of confirmation bias since at least the time of the ancient Greeks. Thucydides said, 'for it is a habit of humanity to entrust to careless hope what they long for, and to use sovereign reason to thrust aside what they do not'.

However, the real work of understanding this bias started in the 1960s with the work of Peter Wilson. He coined the term *confirmation bias* following a series of laboratory-based experiments.

Confirmation bias is simply the tendency to look for data supporting our prior views and beliefs. It can actively work against us – causing us to disregard or 'thrust aside', as Thucydides put it, anything that challenges our assumptions.

Generally, when confirmation bias is at work, we become far more closed-minded. We also become far more convinced that we're right – even if we're not.

The risk for us is once we have formed an opinion about something, we tend to find growing support for it. We reject and ignore any information that doesn't support our view.

Again, it's a way for us to conserve energy and critical brain power. After all, it's far easier to search for information on something we've already thought about than on something that we've not yet considered.

Confirmation bias can lead us to overestimate the frequency of events or even the causal links between things occurring.

What's interesting when dealing with someone suffering from confirmation bias is that giving them an opposing view rarely helps them 'see' otherwise. They already have the proof they need.

Confirmation bias can work similarly in different ways: from believing that left-handed people are more creative than right-handed people to racial and gender discrimination.

So, if you can't simply add additional information into the mix to overcome this, then what do you do?

To protect ourselves against confirmation bias, we should understand why, from a psychological perspective, it occurs.

Generally, it's accepted that there are two possible causes of confirmation bias: motivational and cognitive errors.

Research at Princeton University compared the two against each other, and in the process, came to an understanding of how to overcome this tricky little bias.

Motivational causes of confirmation bias tend to be most common when people notice information that supports their prior beliefs and worldview. Or it could show up in stereotypes or large generalisations.

The other form of confirmation bias is more subtle. It's known as the cognitive form of confirmation bias, or the unmotivated form. It stems from not asking the right questions about new information.

It is, in essence, incorrect reasoning. This is much more complicated than the motivational form because there could be many reasons why we do not reason correctly, from logic mistakes to memory limitations.

In a follow-up study, the biased assimilation experiment was re-run. In the process, they tested two types of instructions as to how people would handle evidence about the effectiveness of the death penalty as a deterrent factor for the crime of murder.

Two groups were created: the motivational group and the cognition group.

The instructions for the motivational group instructed them to be as unbiased and objective as possible. They had to see themselves as a juror and treat all the evidence impartially and fairly.

For the cognition group, the instructions did not state what the desired outcome should be but gave them a strategy they had to use. 'Ask yourself at each step whether you would have made the same high or low evaluations had exactly the same study produced results on the other side of the issue.'

If they were given research that indicated that the death penalty resulted in a lower number of murders, they were asked to examine that research method and to consider whether the opposite results could be more correct. This is nicknamed 'consider the opposite' strategy.

The motivational theory group showed the same biases when they considered the evidence as in the first experiment. In other words, their preconceived ideas carried through the day. Even though they had to be 'impartial and fair', the pro-death participants saw the evidence as supporting the death penalty while the anti-death penalty supporters saw it as supporting abolition.

The participants who had to consider the opposite viewpoints overcame their biased assimilation effect. They remained neutral and didn't rate any of the evidence or studies in a more extreme light, be it pro or against.

The results provided good support for our faith in human nature. It seems that it is not that we don't want to find the truth in a situation, but that we just need a proper strategy to address any given situation or set of information coming at us. This makes us overcome the natural human short-sightedness for considering alternatives.

It should be clear that what underpins better decision-making is not the desire to be objective and fair. That is not sufficient.

We need practical guidelines or strategies to address our limited ability to reason because a major limitation we suffer from is considering alternatives.

If we are lucky, there may be people around to assist us with this but even if there aren't, understanding how the strategy of 'considering the opposite' works should stand us in good stead the next time we have to address unfamiliar situations.[136]

Availability bias & recency effect

Another cognitive trap we find ourselves in is the availability bias.

We typically misjudge events that we find easy to recall as being far more frequent than they actually are.

The example that Marx and Weber gave us was that of thunderstorms. In an experiment that led to the 2013 paper 'Decision Making Under Climate Uncertainty', they simply asked participants: are thunderstorms more frequent in July or August?

Their answer was typically the one that they could more easily recall.

'Whichever category provides more available concrete examples, or for which it feels easier to generate examples, is the one that is judged to be more likely.'[137]

The risk this bias brings with it should be pretty obvious.

Just as with confirmation bias, our thinking can quickly get pretty skewed. In turn, the conclusions we arrive at about how frequently something happens ends up bearing little relation to reality.

We can completely misjudge the frequency with which something happens.

In previous chapters, we have talked about why people miss change. Why do we expect the current status quo to continue almost indefinitely into the future? Availability bias holds an illuminating light.

Availability bias helps us make quick decisions and rough calculations based on the frequency we've seen things happen.

We must remember that when talking about disruptive innovation, progress is not smooth. There are periods – transitional periods – where change is far quicker than usual.

As the innovation cycle lasts around fifty years, our personal experience of these different phases is limited.

In turn, our ability to recall such times is hard. We extrapolate this to mean that radical change in the future is not only unlikely, but improbable. Is this view a biased misjudgement? History would suggest so.

We also need to consider the *recency effect* here. Things that have occurred more recently also appear to us at a cognitive level to occur more frequently.

This can cause us to be blind to infrequent but significant events, not only innovation-related change but also natural events, wars, and rebellions.

Max and Webber once again give us a great example.

While we all have ideas about how the future may look, our most easily recalled life experience is the here and now. It is the most visceral. For most people, this is also the vision that extrapolates into the future. *Sure, the world will be different in twenty years – but not that different. Will it?*

Cass Sunstein, professor at Harvard University and founder of their behavioural economics programme, put the recency effect into an example of climate change.

Essentially, those living in areas that are not affected by climate change do not have experience of the change occurring and therefore are less able to bring forward examples of it. From what we understand about availability bias, this leads us to under-weigh the probability of climate change occurring in the future and overestimate the likelihood that life carries on 'as is' because it's far easier to recall these situations.

Of course, it is not just climate change that this relates to. We tend to downplay the probability of any event that hasn't personally affected us (e.g., the technological shifts we have been discussing) from occurring in the future.

The final reason this bias causes us to misjudge frequency is that information we most recently received can also be deemed to have more weight. It's easy to recall.

Therefore, when we hear stories of child abductions, airplane crashes, or a financial market crisis, we become convinced that their frequency in the future will be increased too.

As we saw with the confirmation bias above, simply knowing about the bias isn't usually enough to overcome it. The same is valid with availability bias and recency effect. Instead, we need a more strategic approach that makes us shift our thought patterns and consider new data.

We have to slow down.

One way to do this is to simply consider the facts about a situation. This strategy is based on the adage: the best antidote to uncertainty is knowledge.

If we apply this to the fear of flying, a common worry among many people, and look at plane crash statistics, we will find there is a very low chance of this occurring.

So low that Dr. Arnold Bennett, Professor of Statistics at the Massachusetts Institute of Technology (MIT) said this: 'A person would have to fly on average once a day every day for 22,000 years before they would die in a US commercial airplane accident according to recent accident rates'.

The use of heuristics and biases when considering the future

Although biases and heuristics can be dangerous in certain circumstances, leading to pitfalls in our thinking, they can also help shorten decision-making time.

We all have to make decisions and infer judgements hourly, if not by the minute.

At the same time, the amount of data and information we're confronted with is virtually infinite.

Because our mental capacity is limited, heuristics come into play as a strategy for reducing complexity and achieving results that, even if not optimal, are satisfactory. Therefore, our aim should not be to rid ourselves of these shortcuts completely but to develop ways of avoiding their most significant pitfalls.

While we'll look at how we do this in the next chapter, we must ensure we build enough opportunities to pause, reflect, and be open to alternative views.

Heuristics can, in fact, be beneficial when used in the correct situation. Consider our previous discussion on scenarios or foresight. The scenario method is one of the best foresight methods. The common understanding is that the scenario approach 'provides a systematic process of creating alternative pictures of the future'.[138]

Because scenarios are descriptions of plausible futures, they rely heavily on heuristics. It's a method for handling uncertainty and complexity.

Building in opportunities to stand back and reflect on the quality of our thinking is also essential, as is avoiding groupthink and incorporating external and differing views.[139]

In the next chapter, we'll consider how heuristics and intuitive thinking can be used to assist us instead of holding us back.

Chapter 16

When Intuition Triumphs

∞

In the last chapter, we outlined two of the most common biases we need to be aware of when thinking about the world around us.

We outlined it from the perspective that taking shortcuts routinely causes unwanted errors in our decision-making and judgement and that this way of thinking can hold us back from uncovering the truth of a situation. We've seen how they negatively skew our thinking or throw us off-course, particularly when looking to the future.

While this is true, it is not the case that all heuristics, mental shortcuts, and even intuition are things we should seek to avoid.

In correcting the biases already outlined, we want to actively embrace and enhance our intuitive ability. Our gut feeling can quickly discern change and point us in the right direction to discover more.

Capturing the zeitgeist

It is not uncommon for writers, musicians, and other artists to pick up on the deeper streams of change and the submerged feelings of the times they live in. They're usually hyper-observant people.

They are curious to understand the driving forces of the world around them, even if they only grasp it subconsciously and hold little technical understanding to explain what they see other than through their work.

At the start of the twentieth century, Mary Shelly's book, *Frankenstein*, perfectly picked up on the fear and trepidation of society regarding this new discovery called 'electricity'.

Andy Warhol is credited with the observation long before the advent of social media networks, or even the internet, that: 'In the future, everyone will be world-famous for 15 minutes'.

In the 1950s, a new style of music, rock and roll, entered the scene and resonated with the young post-war baby generation that was becoming the new consumer. Parents were, on the whole, horrified by this new style of music – labelling it decidedly unchristian and devil music. But it spoke aptly of the change afoot.

More recently, the works of Banksy have captured the feeling of our time with his painting on canvas called *Devolved Parliament* depicting the UK house of parliament filled with chimps, rather than ministers. It spoke of the unorganised chaos that much of the public felt about the antiquated system. He'd originally painted it in 2002, but its relevance grew instead of shrinking away, re-selling at the height of the Brexit drama for £9.9m.

In these examples, I am not suggesting that these artists knew what was coming or that they could see it. But instead, they could sense it. Changes at a societal level, as we've already looked at, take a long time to play out, and for those more in tune with the world around them, the slow, long-tails of barely perceptible change at the fringes are all that is needed to glean insights.

Iowa gambling task

The Iowa gambling task highlights this point perfectly. In an experiment, participants were presented with four decks of cards and told that the aim of the game is to figure out the best strategy to win money. When turned over, some cards won money; some lost. In essence, the participants had to choose from which deck they would draw the next card.

What the participants didn't know was that two of the decks were rigged. They'd been put together with far more 'bad' money-losing cards. If they drew too heavily from these, they'd quickly see their rate of winning money decline and their rate of losing money increase. But they didn't know anything was rigged.

Most participants started with a similar strategy. Take a few cards from each deck and get a feel for which might be the key to success. After forty or fifty cards were drawn, more people had made up their mind, stuck with good decks, and continued to draw on these for the rest of the game.

But what the neurologist Antonie Bechara and his team were also keen on finding out was what was going on below the conscious level. Did the hunch that there were good and bad decks occur at the same time subconsciously and consciously?

Measuring the galvanic skin response of the participants, which detects an early stress response, they found something astonishing. While the participants had consciously found out which decks were good or bad after fifty cards or so, they had subconsciously started to make this inference way before. Based on their stress response, some had intuitively sensed something was up with the two decks after just ten cards.

For Bechara, he was more interested in these results from the perspective of how those with damaged regions of the brain, specifically the ventromedial prefrontal cortex, performed and whether this affected how well they made decisions in real-life situations compared to those with normal functions.[140]

But for us, it starts to provide a little insight into the speed and ability of our unconscious intelligence.

All thinking is ultimately subconscious

Gerd Gigerenzer is one researcher who has dedicated much of his career to what he refers to as 'fast and frugal' heuristics. Fast because they don't take us an eternity to reach a conclusion, and frugal because they help us conserve cognitive energy. These are the kind of mental shortcuts, or rules of thumb, that we can use to assist us and lead us to make more accurate, less-taxing decisions in the real world and in complex environments.

One of the things we learn from Gigerenzer's work is that nearly all information is, in fact, processed subconsciously. That might sound obvious. But it stands in contrast to how we're encouraged to think. Most schools support slow, rational, deliberate thought processes and shun the idea of intuitive understanding. As we looked at in the last chapter, the entire neoclassical school of economics is built on the assumption that we, as *homoeconomucus*, carefully collect all possible data, lay it out, assess, and weigh the benefits and costs.

However, research increasingly shows that our thought processes are always grounded in unconscious intelligence. It is, after all, the unconscious mind that ultimately decides what information you will take into account, what you will notice, and what you pay attention and hold on to.

While we can, and should, consciously check our thinking from time to time to ensure that the information we're using is not overly biased – our subconscious is always working in the background.

Embracing the subconscious can work well in the real world.

But, again, here we find a lot of the research suggesting that rational processing is superior to inference. The issue with much of this research is it comes from laboratory-style experiments that control the level of complexity and only provide artificial randomness.

In the real world, where there is an abundance of data, intuition-based strategies can be highly accurate and effective. In fact, the two environments we commonly find ourselves in are ones where we have little to no knowledge of the subject, or we know so much that to compute all the information we know in a rational and systematic way would be impossibly tiring. But what if this slow and diligent method was also less accurate?

Let's start with environments where we have very little information. This is where *the recognition heuristic* can help us make decisions that we'd have little idea how to solve at a rational level. In everyday language, we'd typically label these as lucky guesses, but we shouldn't be so quick to dismiss them as pure chance or simple fate. On many occasions, there's a lot more going on – we're searching our information archives for something, anything, that matches.

Let me give you an example. Which German city has the larger population? Munich or Dortmund?

Paradoxically, for those with little knowledge of German cities, the answer might jump out at you more than someone who knows these cities well.

It was this observation that encouraged Gigerenzer to dig deeper. This didn't make sense. So, what was going on?

While lecturing at the University of Saltsburg, Gigerenzer developed the theory of recognition heuristic while asking his German students about the population of two American cities. Once again, he found that the German students were correct more of the time about the

American cities than they were about their own German ones.

Quite simply, the fact that the German students had little information on the populations of the American cities helped them. It meant that instead of slowly and consciously working their way through all the data, counting up the number of neighbourhoods, schools, whether both had football clubs, universities, and so on – they could ask a far easier question. Which one had they heard of?

This was enough: it was a good enough proxy to choose the right answer.

But the recognition heuristic isn't available as soon as you know about the topic or subject. So, what do you do then?

Here, Gigerenzer and Goldstein had a similar breakthrough. This time, they use the take-the-best heuristic to focus your attention on the best attribute that discriminates between choices.

Let's say you're trying to evaluate how safe a particular flight is. You have knowledge of both airline carriers, so you can't use the recognition heuristic, and both have very similar safety records.

Perhaps the next thing you could focus on is the experience of the pilots – if both are equal, then maybe you move on to the plane's age. Finding out that one is five years old and the other is forty-five years old, you may conclude that the older one comes with more risk.

In this instance, you have gone with the best piece of information. Instead of asking for a list of all variables and using some kind of regression analysis, you've chosen the best piece of information and based your decision on that.

Sure, this is quick and straightforward, but is this really accurate in the real world? I mean, come on.

That is exactly what the research is suggesting. Researchers Armstrong and Graefe decided to test this in the real world. They used the take-the-best heuristic in the field of political forecasting and compared the results from this to more traditional forecasting techniques, such as those using econometric models and regression analysis. Not only did the take-the-best heuristic stand up to these rigorous forecasting techniques, but it also yielded an accurate forecast rate of ninety-seven per cent.[141]

Patterns of change

Alongside *fast and frugal* heuristics, we also come across the work of Gary Klein, who formed his research around what he calls *naturalistic decision making*. Klein's research, like that of Goldstein and Gigerenzer, deviates from the rational decision-making camps and holds a far more positive view of humans' abilities to make fast and accurate intuitive decisions. This is not to say that fast and frugal heuristics and natural decision-making camps see eye to eye on everything. They don't.

In recent years, a small number of decision researchers have suggested that there could be an integration, but research has remained limited.

Klein's work offers us additional insight in his focus on how expertise affects intuition. For much of his career, Klein has been focused on this group. Klein started noticing experts from various fields, including first responders, military commanders, helicopter pilots, firefighters, and doctors were picking up on subtle clues and signs that others were not. Using these signals, their intuitive decision-making leapt forward, and to many casual observers, it was the appearance of a sixth sense, or extrasensory perception.

Intuition is the use of patterns they've already learned, whereas insight is the discovery of new patterns

– Gary Klein

After Klein's suggestion to Gigerenzer that fast and frugal heuristics could benefit from an increased focus on expertise, Gigerenzer and others incorporated this into their research. They concluded that experts did differ from novices – they could search through information faster and used less cognitive power to get there.[142]

At the heart of naturalistic decision making is the idea of building intuition. Unlike the fast and frugal heuristics, intuition here is about becoming more familiar with patterns and with how things typically play out – becoming an expert.

What the expert has that the novice doesn't is thousands of patterns that allow them to identify small clues of deviation and change quickly and efficiently. It's these and the insights they gain from them that seem to be one of the reasons they respond so well.

As most of you will know, there was a rule of thumb uncovered by Ander Ericsson, psychology professor at Florida State University, that you need to put in ten thousand hours of diligent practice before becoming an expert.[143] While the amount of time will vary from discipline to discipline and be affected by how hard the practice is and how good the teaching is, it makes sense in light of what Klein is suggesting.

Conclusion

In this section, we have looked at the structure of the environment in which we make decisions and take on information. These environments can skew how we see things, think about things, and can affect our core values and worldview.

We have considered both sides: our biases can bring flaws in our decision-making, and we need to adopt a slower, more deliberate, rational thought process. But there are also times and situations where that's not always the case. I am suggesting that we adopt a far more pragmatic approach. Sometimes we would be right to harness the quicker and more efficient ways brought about by intuition.

Suppose my view is correct. Then, over time, we will see these schools of thought – the heuristics and biases, fast and frugal, and naturalistic decision making – find more synergy and be applied more coherently. Each offers rich insights into decision-making under conditions of uncertainty and can be applied deliberately at different points of the learning and decision-making process, therefore, one should not be too hasty to subscribe to just one.

In this sense, we should not shy away from intuitive decision-making. Even if much of society, especially traditional education systems, encourage us to only think in slower and more deliberative ways. For too long the intuitive ways of thinking have been shunned as unscientific in search of a purely logical, rational, cost-benefit methods.

Not only is current research highlighting that intuition can be just as good, but in the real world – in the big world outside of fixed-risk laboratory experiments using students that have little experience – it can be superior.

This is not too much of a surprise when we consider the processing power we neglect if we solely choose the conscious rational side of our brains. Our conscious brain can process just a fraction of what our subconscious can, with some studies suggesting that the processing power of the subconscious is many thousands of times faster.

The key to utilising this, as we've looked at throughout this book, is learning to dip below the noise and find richer streams of information beyond the hype.

Section Three

Collective Progress

In this last section, I want to touch on something that I feel is vital to our continued progress as a human race.

That's a big statement – but the challenges we have up ahead, not only from climate change but also from an ageing population, debt saturation, and shifting global forces, require us to come together and co-operate like never before.

On the point of climate change, I believe, from the research I have seen and the innovation coming through, that there is still plenty to be optimistic for. There are in fact many reasons to believe that the innovation occurring today will do more than overcome these hurdles. It could well bring about a new golden age.

The transition from a carbon-based economy however is not one to be taken lightly. Much of our economic progress has been centred on increasing production through harnessing and extracting energy more efficiently.

Decoupling this without also decoupling the advancements and innovation is a delicate matter.

Unfortunately, many people do not have a good understanding of how innovation works.

You now have a framework – and with this, sit in a privileged position. But those without such understanding, caught up in the hype of the mass media and hysteria of click-bait news, wrongly attribute blame and cause.

In this final section, I make a case for why we need to adopt a far more positive view of both human nature and the capitalist system that allows the creative side of our human nature – our innovative nature – to shine through.

The imperative for this has never been greater.

Chapter 17

Restoring Human Good

∞

Nothing is more common than the assumption that without a state, a society will fall necessarily and immediately into violent disorder; indeed, anarchy and chaos are often used as synonyms

– Robert Higgs[144]

Throughout history, philosophers have warned us about the underlying dark side of our human nature. That we should be careful who we talk with. Even more, we should be careful what we do for others as they could be using us to further their own gains.

But is this narrative true?

Just ask yourself if this view reflects the world you know. Not the wider world that you only see through the lens of other people's stories or the mass media. But ask it of your own world. Of the people directly around you – perhaps your household or your street.

The more familiar you are with the people you think of, and the closer the link you have with them, does this idea become more favourable or less?

For most people, when they focus on the people they know, the ones living in closest proximity, their view of the kindness of the world lifts significantly.

We understand these people, their humanity, and their stories. Most people would say their own neighbourhood is far kinder than the world is on average.

This occurs just as in the psychology experiment that asks people to state whether they felt their driving was above or below average. Of course, overwhelmingly most of us think our own driving is far better than average!

Over the years, there have been many examples of what we call the superiority illusion, or the better-than-average bias.

In fact, it shows up in so many aspects of life, from overstating our height to understating our weight. But this also shows up in the self vs. aggregate arena – and the familiar vs. unfamiliar arena. In other words, we are far more likely to rank ourselves, and the people we associate with, as far *better* than the world on aggregate.

But our dim view of human nature is not just about this internal bias to overvalue our attributes. Over the years, this has also been a narrative put on us – intentionally or not.

The phrase 'survival of the fittest' conjures up in most people's minds the image of physical dominance and superiority that is unleashed on lesser beings.

In the corporate sense, we think of business owners who mistreat their staff just to increase the bottom line. Charles Dickens's *A Christmas Carol* depicts this very essence in the character of Ebenezer Scrooge.

Darwin's theory of evolution is typically told in the sense that the strongest and the most cutthroat player wins.

In both cases, success came at the expense of those at the bottom.

Human nature: altruistic or selfish?

Understanding the basic human disposition, attributes, and nature has been a constant debate throughout our civilization's history.

Over the years, philosophers and social scientists have put forward different political and philosophical assumptions.

However, some of these great philosophers saw us (humans) through a very primitive lens. Many believing we are selfish and wicked and would do anything to survive, even if we had to put others down. In this view, we are not capable of living without crisis.

Others however believed that we could love, exhibit selflessness, and live peacefully with those around us.

Prominent in these assumptions are two historical heavy-weights: Thomas Hobbes and Jean-Jacques Rousseau.

It's worth us looking at their thoughts on human nature, their political disposition, and their influence on our society today.

Thomas Hobbes, an English philosopher in the sixteenth century, was interested in how humans could live in harmony and avoid the danger and horror of civil war. Hobbes believed that humans are, in their heart, inherently greedy.

According to him, if humans were to be left to live freely (i.e., without any governance), humans would constantly conflict with each other. In this free state, Hobbes surmised that a man's life was 'lonely, poor, ugly, wretched, and fleeting'.

To Hobbes, peace was something precious – but fleeting and fragile. People need to answer to a state. They needed to be governed.

In his bid to solve this problem, he offers a number of solutions. According to Hobbes, we should give up our freedom and submit to an unchecked ruler (an individual authorised to determine every social and political matter). Otherwise, we will be in the midst of a civil war before we know it.

Hobbes also felt that any attempt at making a government more answerable to the people would undermine it. It would also put the country in perilous danger of entering a state of *non-governance*: which in Hobbes's view, we want to avoid at all costs.

As a result, according to Hobbes, our only viable choice is a 'sovereign' government that is entirely unaccountable to its people.

On the other hand, Jean-Jacques Rousseau, a Geneva-born philosopher who came much after Hobbes, had an opposing view of human nature.

Contrary to Hobbes's belief, Rousseau described man as one born to be free. He held the true nature of man's freedom as enviable absolute freedom: physically, psychologically, and spiritually.

He sided with the view that humans should never be forced to give up their natural rights to a sovereign ruler. He observed that in man's free state, the challenge was to find a way to preserve everyone's life, freedom, and possessions while yet allowing them to be free.

Rousseau's solution was for humans to hand over all their rights to 'the whole community', or all the people, rather than a single ruler.

He referred to everyone as 'sovereign'. The people would then use their 'collective will' to enact laws for the 'common good'.

Furthermore, he contended that elected politicians could not decide on the broad will of the people. He firmly believed in a true democracy, where everyone casts a vote to represent the public will and make laws.

Rousseau's vision was at the heart of the foundation of the United States of America, with its liberalist positioning that upholds equality and individual liberty. It can also be seen in the strict rule of law over private property and a limited constitutional government.

Even the very start of the US constitution begins with the words 'we the people', echoing the sentiment of Rousseau's view on popular sovereignty.

Sadly, in our society today, we've edged towards a more Hobbesian view of humanity. Supporting larger governments and increasing control over people's lives, predicated on the theory that if we didn't have a ruler over us, we'd devolve into anarchy.

But anarchy is not our default.

As a human race, we have exhibited selfless characters, put aside selfish interests, and upheld those of our compatriots first. A look at the history of humankind finds that one of man's core attributes is his social ability.

We're capable of living peacefully with others, helping others, and avoiding conflicts. If an individual enacts violence and harm against another, then generally, they are accountable to the rest of the tribe, village, town, state, or government.

This does not always occur the other way around – when a government does harm.

Max Weber, the founder of Sociology, felt strongly on this point. He saw government, certainly one that gained too much power, as one of the biggest threats to humanity.

Weber defined the state as a 'community that claims the monopoly of the legitimate use of physical force within a given territory'.

The terms *monopoly* and *legitimate* Webber used are the two key terms here. Monopoly is not suggesting that the state – or government – is the only one that uses force, but rather, it's the only one that can legitimise such action.

The list of mass genocides in the past hundred years at the hands of power-hungry governments is a sad testament to this fact.

Altruistic

As the Covid-19 pandemic hit, a Hobbesian view predicted that we would quickly sink into our 'ugly, wretched, and poor' selves.

However, instead of acting selfishly and trampling on our fellow citizens to get an edge, the opposite occurred.

Sure, there were a select few individuals that trampled on others to get the last packs of toilet rolls in supermarkets, but on the whole, the globe began to deliberately go out of its way to assist its fellow citizens.

We saw altruism rise in every part of the world as individuals put aside racial, religious, and political differences to combat a common enemy that threatened their existence.

Hobbes wouldn't have believed this could ever happen. But it did.

Today, contemporary research suggests that holding an overly pessimistic view of human nature is no longer valid.

Several studies from around the world confirm this. A recent survey conducted across European countries in 2020 by Kings' College London, examined human behaviour as the Covid-19 virus ravaged countries. The result of the study found a significant rise in altruism among the people.

'Altruism, fairness, and social trust are all crucial factors in a prosperous and well-functioning society. The impact of the Covid-19 pandemic on the economy and trades of nations had little or no effect on the behaviour of humans around the world. These findings support the idea that crises that occur among humans improve unity amidst them.'[145]

But why does it matter?

Well, how we see our fellow man influences our view of diversity as well as how we see the role of government. Seeing others in a truly dim light typically motivates us to call for more intervention, more measures, and more controls. Our views presume that 'others' are, after all, unruly and out to get us.

When enough people think this way, power is duly handed over, with greater sovereignty granted to the ruling party. Of course, this initially appears to be to our benefit.

New rules, laws, and regulations make those minor tweaks we wanted. Incentives are put in place to 'correct' the behaviour we believe others need. But rarely does it stop there.

With ever more issues on the horizon, the governments cry goes out that they could do more – if only they had a little more money and resources, a little more power.

Governments are not a generative force of economic production, but simply a redistributive one. Neither is the government a free service. Therefore, for the government to get bigger, its need to tax and borrow also grows.

Over the years, many have claimed that the money taken out of the economy through taxation can be carefully re-circulated to the areas of the economy and society that need it the most.

Keynes, the British economist, went as far as to say that government spending comes with a multiplier effect. That is, somehow, when the government spends a pound, a dollar, a euro, or a yen, it is worth far more.

This theory has been a key justification for increased government spending far more frequently than you may imagine. I also assume that the government officials believe it to be true.

Unfortunately, while Keynes' idea was a nice one, there is little suggestion that it occurs in the real world.

There is, however, reason to believe that the government multiplier effect is, in fact, quite the opposite.

The standard view – supported by the government at least – is that periods of increased government spending lead to periods of increased economic expansion. But if we dig into the data, this isn't quite what we find.

In 1999, four researchers put together a working paper for the National Bureau of Economic Research. Their focus was on fiscal policy – that is, government spending and taxation – and the effects of this on corporate profits and investment levels.

What they found was that increases in public spending and government intervention held a negative effect on the profits of corporations. In turn, this led to lower levels of investment.

The evidence didn't suggest that there was a *multiplier effect* at work. Quite the opposite. Instead, their suggestion was that government spending and intervention hindered future growth, innovation, and future prosperity.

Am I calling for the end of government?

Not exactly. I'm just saying that we shouldn't naively support ever expansive levels of government intervention.

We still need the government. Just a smaller one that concentrates its efforts on upholding the rule of law and maintains an independent judicial system. Beyond that, and a few public goods and services, I question it.

If men were angels

Let's first make a distinction. My appeal in this chapter is that you see human nature in a more positive light, which typically leads to greater levels of collaboration, community, and that all-important factor of collective intelligence.

This is very different from me asking you to believe that humans are only capable of doing good. Our experience of the world shows otherwise.

If we believed that others were infallible, then we would not need a government. Instead, there would be a perfect state of self-governance.

James Madison, Fourth President of the United States of America, made a similar observation: 'if men were angels, no government would be necessary. If angels were to govern man, neither external nor internal controls on government would be necessary'.

Given that we're not angelic all the time, we end up with a similar conundrum to Madison.

'The great difficulty lies in this: you must first enable a government to control the governed; and in the next place oblige it to control itself'. James Madison, Federalist No. 51, 1788

This issue is brought into stark focus at the time of writing this book. In the UK, there are new enquiries over the current prime minister, Boris Johnson, and the lockdown parties that ensued under his watch. The rules he'd ushered in and enforced on the public appeared not to hold for himself.

While this might appear a simple case of double standards and seem inconsequential – there are plenty of examples where governments' *unjust* rule is far more dangerous.

One rule for one, and one for another.

The other observation we should note is that once governments assume more power, rarely is it reduced.

Economic Historian Dr. Robert Higgs uncovered what he called the Ratchet Effect. Higgs looked at the growth of government, how it leaped forward during times of crisis, and how it only partially receded afterwards.

Over time, this leads to a significant growth of government power, influence, and intervention.

Perhaps the most important function of the government, or state, is upholding the rule of law.

This rests as a centrepiece of human achievement, innovation, and prosperity. Bizarrely as a concept, however, it is hardly ever found in economic textbooks.

The key to understanding the rule of law is to think about it like this. It protects me from you, and you from me: we are both governed and accountable to the same laws, applied in the same way. It is the set of rules that protect both private property rights, and also lays out the rules by which life is to be lived.

To uphold laws justly is the need for an independent judicial system that applies these laws in an unbiased and transparent way.

This was the call from the protestors in Hong Kong. Their fear was that greater interference in Hong Kong law would not only alter the laws to favour the government but would bring down the independent application of these laws too.

Where countries have a strong rule of law, coupled with a strong independent judicial system, we typically see a correlation with economic progress, innovation, and quality of life. It fosters an environment where entrepreneurial spirit can flourish.

Taking the opposite environment: for countries that have a low level of rule of law, such as Venezuela, Cambodia, and the Democratic Republic of Congo, there is little hope of economic progress.

The very real risk in these environments is anything you spend time and money creating could be taken away, plundered, or stolen without recourse.

The hurdles humanity has ahead surrounding climate change, debt levels, and demographic challenges requires collective action and innovation. Slipping backwards through the inefficient allocation of resources and bigger governments will not only cause economic stagnation in the future – but may even risk the future of humanity.

The World Justice Project, which produces an annual report based on their Rule of Law Index, highlighted in the 2020 report that of the 128 countries they looked at, 'more countries declined than improved in the overall rule of law for a third year in a row'.[146]

Chapter 18

Disenchanted with Capitalism

∞

In early 2021, a new phrase started trending on TikTok and Twitter: *Eat the Rich.*

Kids armed with forks were showing up in videos talking of the injustice they saw in the gap between the *haves* and *have-nots* – which in their view was getting wider.

Much wider.

It was simply unacceptable.

While there was plenty of fork waving at those on the world's rich lists, even those with mild luxuries of say 'two fridges' or an 'electric gate' were in the firing line too.

The echo chambers of social media that we looked at back in an earlier chapter served to amplify their message, and calls to their networks of followers to unfollow celebrities or anyone with a *start button* on their car quickly grew in number.

At the same time, rallies were popping up with similar slogans: *capitalism = inequality* and *capitalism has failed us*. These phrases flew high on 20-foot banners, and the people that carried them felt it captured the root cause of their situation.

Calls such as these are not necessarily all that new.

They've occurred at similar points in each of the previous technological waves. Laying the blame of inequality at the feet of capitalism goes in cycles.

My suggestion? It's less about capitalism and more about the stage of the innovation cycle we find ourselves at.

In some periods, capitalism is the facilitating force that solves inequality, raises the general level of prosperity, and furthers our medical ability – and with it, our quality of life.

Discontentment and disenchantment with capitalism typically rises at the point when the paradigm-shifting technology of the era reaches the point of mass adoption.

Today, digitalisation has become the norm. It has become mass adopted. And as such those we find atop the rich list are typically the ones who had some role in bringing this paradigm about: or have harnessed its productive might in their investments or businesses.

Of course, there were many others – founders, inventors, and investors who 'backed the wrong horse' – who put their time and money behind the wrong technology.

As the leading technology of the day reaches maturity, the earning power of businesses that best harness it rises significantly.

Compare this to the earning potential of businesses that are the *stars* of past innovation waves. Today we could look back at companies engaged in heavy engineering, oil, gas, railways, airlines, shipping, utilities, and so on. They were the corporate superstars of decades past.

While all these past superstars might 'upgrade' their businesses to utilise the new technology, their core production system remains tied to previous waves of innovation.

ExxonMobil certainly uses digital tools to assist in its operations, but it can't shake the fact that it's still predominantly an oil business.

Compare this to a company like Microsoft – a business that derives its revenues from the current technology wave of innovation.

The investors in these two firms have seen very different returns. In the past ten years, between 2012 and 2022, Microsoft has seen its share value increase by nearly a thousand per cent, whereas Exxon? A little over twenty-five per cent.

This is not to say that Exxon is unimportant – not at all. Its core technology, however, is rooted in a previous wave: the oil industry, which boomed in the early 1900s.

This isn't just about investors' returns; its impact touches countless other areas. Wages can quickly become stagnant in an industry that has seen its heyday. Job security can also take a nosedive.

If we turn our focus to history, we find numerous examples. The rise of the railways led to the decline in use of horses – as well as the industries that existed to support horse drawn transport: vets, stables, carriage makers, farriers, and so on.

Those finding themselves on the side of these declining industries saw their wealth, at least relatively, tumble compared to those in the new-fangled railways and mills.

This time around, the growing discontentment has been building visibly since the 2000s, coinciding with the rise of a mass adoption of new information technology and digitalisation.

Also fanning the flames of talk about inequality are influential studies such as those from the Levy Institute. Edward Wolff in July 2009 commented, ‘median wealth plunged by 36 percent and there was a fairly steep rise in wealth inequality’. Wolf went on to say that the Gini coefficient in 2009, for the US, stood at 0.865.[147] Basically, that’s high. Very high.

The Gini coefficient tries to tell us just how severe the wealth disparity is. It runs on a scale of 0 to 1: where zero equals complete equality, and one represents complete inequality.

By 2013, it wasn’t just academics shouting about this either, President Obama was echoing this sentiment calling inequality ‘the defining issue of our time’.[148]

As mentioned, there is a regularity and cyclicality to this type of anti-capitalistic view. Often, the main arguments are that capitalism supports – and is even the root cause of – inequality.

More recently, there have been new ideological attacks. These turn their focus to climate change and social responsibility, once again claiming that capitalism is unfit for the job at hand. We are told that to tackle climate change, we need degrowth, and to improve social responsibility, we need a better system that is, well, more moral.

We'll come back to these claims because they're as essential as they are worrying in the conclusions they draw.

In this book, I have presented an optimistic view of the road ahead. My optimism is not rooted in naivety, but rather rests on an understanding of just how innovative and creative we, the human race, can be – and have shown ourselves to be over the past few centuries.

There is a caveat to this optimism, however. It's based on the assumption that we continue to live in a world where the mechanisms of progress – the entrepreneurial spirit that free markets foster – are supported.

In the previous chapter, we looked at the role of the political sphere in this – that if the government assumes too big a role, starts spending more, raises taxes too high, and intervenes in places it shouldn't, the beating heart of innovation and progress starts to significantly slow.

With the severity of the challenges ahead, I don't believe we have the luxury of stalling innovation.

In this chapter, I turn to the capitalist structure as one that in my view, we need to do more to build up, rather than tear down. This is a socially sensitive topic. Being pro-capitalism is almost as hated by certain groups as suggesting that we are heading to the next golden age. In part because it's often confused with being pro-inequality and pro-natural destruction. Both things are not necessarily true.

So, let's start with the basics. Capitalism is not perfect. After all, it's a system made up of billions of individuals – and while I suggest we have encouragingly good characteristics, none of us are perfect.

What we need to understand is that in direct opposition to other competing systems, capitalism is a system that promotes freedom, social mobility, general prosperity, and undeniable innovation. Other systems don't do that – despite their early promises and campaign slogans.

Sure, there are periods when capitalism is not cast in the best light, particularly when the newly rich parade their wealth around, ignorant of the fact others at the same time are finding themselves in industries that have questionable futures. But when we consider what system can raise the general standard of living, and give future generations the best possible future world, capitalism is the one you want.

In fact, when considering the history of human progress, capitalism has outperformed all other competing systems, including socialism, communism, and authoritarianism by a considerable margin.[149] As the saying goes: *capitalism creates inequality, socialism creates poverty.*

Before we look at a definition of capitalism, and what it is and what it isn't, let's come back to the point on inequality – starting from where we've come from. Because while the rich have gotten richer, the poor have got considerably richer too.

Just a few centuries ago, most families around the world lived on the breadline.

Having children was not so much a luxury of bringing life into the world and experiencing the joy of being a parent, but one of economic necessity to balance the books and bring in enough income to put food on the table. Child labour was an essential family input.

Food and money were so scarce that for some groups, such as the French peasants, it's been suggested that during winter months they would adopt some kind of hibernation to conserve energy.[150]

That's the world that we've rapidly ascended from in just a short couple of centuries.

It's also here that we need to make an important distinction – another socially unpalatable one. While the gap between the rich and poor is undesirable, particularly for those not on the rich list, 'poor' and 'poverty' are very different.

Poverty is something we should absolutely work together to eliminate; great inroads are being made on this front.

Poor is far more relative. In the TikTok-er's case, in general, their echoing of the eighteenth century 'Eat the Rich' was not so much about literally starving at the hands of the ruling elite, as the phrase was initially intended. It was more about not having quite enough for the very fastest broadband package, or latest iPhone so that their videos can be shot in ultra-HD.

So, where does inequality fit into this mix? And do we even want to live in a world where income and wealth are completely equalised?

Or is some level of inequality a far more natural and healthy state than it's commonly purported to be?

Let's go back a bit. In the 1980s, Cuba was, at least from an equality point of view, a pretty good place to set up home. Yet not many in the west would have wanted to trade places. While equal, Cuba was also a place where thousands of its citizens were jailed in appalling conditions, harassed, beaten, intimidated, and denied even the most basic human rights and political freedoms.

Income and wealth inequality are important factors in overall societal happiness, but it's far from being the determinant for quality of life and opportunity.

In fact, having an unequal society suggests that there is a chance of being repaid for hard work. There is the chance of reward for solving others' problems.

The right environment (one that has good rule of law, equality of rights, and supports freedoms) comes with the potential for us to benefit from our work and creativity. We are incentivised to sacrifice and risk our time and capital, and if we do well, others *vote* for our skills, products, and services with their hard-earned cash.

Additionally, if we think outside of setting up in business and making it big, most of us would expect to be in a career or job that comes with the prospect of increasing income as we gain more experience and qualifications. In turn, we'd also expect our older, wiser, more experienced selves to earn more, and have more than our present-day selves.

If you've found yourself agreeing with these things, then the truth is you don't really want a completely equal society.

If you agree with these things, we should take a closer look at some of those research reports on inequality, too. Do they adjust for things like age? Do they consider other important aspects – for instance income being assessed before tax or after tax? And what about transfer payments such as child support and unemployment benefits?

When we start accounting for these items, what we find is that the inequality gap is still there – but it shrinks considerably.[151][152][153]

But what about the excessive pay of CEOs? Surely, this can't be rationalised?

Today, a CEO's pay has increased hundreds of times faster than the average worker.

Xavier Gabaix and Augustin Landier take on this topic, suggesting that there are good reasons why CEOs are earning such high salaries. Companies are getting so much bigger, therefore talent is not just rewarded, but valued even more in this highly globalised economy.

From the data they looked at, they found the pay of CEOs had increased around six times in the twenty or so years leading up to 2003. Remarkably, this was matched by the six times increase in the company's market capitalisation.[154]

Alex Edmans, Professor at London Business School, takes this further, asking why employee pay has lagged so much. His suggestion is in the scalability of talent: CEOs have a *multiplicative* effect, while employees are only *additive*.[155]

This is not to say that things haven't been skewed and distorted. They have. But it's not necessarily originating from inside the business, or due to an inherent flaw in capitalism. Rather this stems from governments and the proto-government body – the central bank.

For several decades, the major central banks have manipulated the cost of money through interest rate policy, quantitative easing, and monetisation of government debt. They would argue that they are working hard to maintain stable prices and a properly functioning economy. That without their intervention, the market would simply fail.

Not only do I strongly disagree with this self-promoted view of central banks being our 'saviours', but I also suggest they cause some other grave issues we see in pay disparity.

Their interest rate manipulation affects risk – specifically investors' risk appetite.

Many companies have been highly innovative and used this to improve the structure and profitability of their businesses. Their stock price, and market capitalisation have duly risen.

But what I'm suggesting is there has also been a secondary tailwind to these increased valuations.

The central bank has reduced the cost of money so far that even risk is under-priced.

How does this relate to CEO pay?

In a word: directly.

Many remuneration packages of CEOs are linked to their firm's market capitalisation.

Its stock price.

So, while their pay can be justified on the additional market value of the business, I'm not so sure it's all their doing.

The central bank, with decades-long policy favouring asset appreciation, has helped considerably.

What is capitalism anyway?

When we actually define capitalism, we see that many of the common objections quickly fall away. That's because most people's objections come from a misunderstanding of what capitalism is, and what it isn't.

The media add to the confusion, with reporting rarely making the distinction between capitalism and something far more insidious – cronyism.

Let's start with cronyism and get this out the way.

The easiest way to think of cronyism is as a corrupt, fraudulent version of capitalism. While on the surface, cronyism appears like capitalism, in reality it rests on companies in bed with government cronies. Favourable regulations, permits, and even tax breaks are granted, and uncompetitive advantages are created for key players.

Of course, some countries have a far higher reputation for cronyism than others, but make no mistake, it happens in nearly all economies at varying levels. It's a life-sucking and highly damaging arrangement.

Russia has been perhaps the poster child for this, with nearly the entire economy of businesses in the government's pocket. But they are by no means alone.

China has had to reinvent its economy after a slew of supposedly privately-owned banks with bad debts had to be made into government entities.

Then we find Argentina, and we see the real cost of cronyism when combined with a big, highly interventionist government: a population that now sees poverty rates at around the forty per cent level.[156] The sad truth of this is with the natural resources Argentina sits on, poverty should never have happened.

With cronyism out of the way, let's move on to capitalism.

One thing that makes it so hard to define exactly what capitalism is comes from the fact that each system is unique. Each capitalist economy is slightly varied, built up around the country's customs and regulations.

Here is, however, the first observation of what capitalism is, and one of its incredible attributes: its ability to be highly adaptable and flexible. This is in stark contrast to, say, centrally planned economies that are extremely rigid.

With so much variance in capitalist economies, perhaps it's best to define it by its characteristics and what capitalist economies share.

When we do this, we find that capitalism is essentially a system where the ownership of production is held in the hands of the individual. In turn, individuals are free to choose what they buy and at what price.

In this environment, when companies fail to meet the needs of the people, their businesses collapse, with consumption going to the ones that better meet the needs of the people. Efficiencies and progress are highly connected to this process.

In the opposite environment, we find that the ownership of production is held in the hands of the ruling elite, either absolutely or through permits.

Instead of people choosing what is produced in an economy through consumption, the ruling elite decide who can set up in business and what products are produced. As such, within controlled economies, what you can buy, and at what price, is not set by market mechanisms of supply and demand but through price control.

In a controlled economy, there is also no mechanism for business failure. This might sound great at first, but over time the centrally controlled system will keep churning unwanted or inefficient stuff despite falling consumer demand.

Why? Because in a controlled economy, it's not the consumer that dictates what is made, but rather the ruling elite prescribing it.

For reasons such as these, the Soviet Union didn't just collapse, but rotted from the inside out.

The other argument made against capitalism is a moral one. But to argue for or against capitalism on a moral basis is again misplaced. The morality rests not with the structure of the economic system, but with the humans who run it.

It is in fact, our not-always perfect nature that means that we should desire to have a system that spreads power and idea generation as wide as possible. Capitalism is the only one that does this by spreading the ownership of production to individuals.

All other economic structures instead concentrate power to smaller and smaller groups of supposedly *good people* who impose their version of utopia on the rest. The issue with this is one person's view of utopia is not the same as another's. Hitler, Stalin, and Mussolini all had utopian visions that in their eyes could be achieved if the rest of the world could just see it.

In a concentrated power system, morality is directly governed by a small group, or even a single person. It assumes we can find a morally perfect, omniscient, omnipresent ruler to rule.

As Allan Melter puts it, the anti-capitalist typically makes three grave mistakes in their thinking. They ignore that because humans are not perfect, power should be spread among as many people as possible – rather than concentrated in a select few.

He also points out that they overlook the simple fact that each of us has different views on what a *perfect* life might look like. Not only does this mean that no single commonly held vision of utopia exists, but a controlled economy also quells creativity, as this is a privileged mindset reserved only for those in charge.

The third mistake? Believing that the appointed leader will remain benevolent and not tyrannical. 'Enforced using fear, terror, prison or punishment. The twentieth century is rife with promised ends that were never realized that turned into justification for deplorable means' Allan Meltzer, Why Capitalism? p. 15.[157]

Capitalism seeks to disperse intelligence, innovation, and risk-taking across as many people as possible. Just as we've seen, societies' understanding and knowledge typically surge forward when information revolutions occur – times when more diverse views and perspectives are considered.

A similar phenomenon seems to also happen in the economy. Free markets that encourage more businesses, innovators, and entrepreneurs to chase their vision leads to higher rates of creativity and breakthroughs.

Socialism, communism, and authoritarianism in varying degrees seek to concentrate power. And, as no humans are omniscient nor infallible, the risks of ruin increase exponentially in line with reduced freedoms.

The countless dystopian movies and books highlight this point well. The focusing of power on just a small group of individuals in society might well promote their narrow view of utopia. But it rarely promotes anything close to utopia for most people below them. For the majority, they are forced to give up free choice to *serve the greater good,* as the dystopian leader often rationalises.

Human nature and our flaws are not inspired by, or the result of, our economic system.

These flaws continue to exist whatever the political and economic regime. History teaches us that moving power toward a small handful of people and away from a free market rarely ends well.

Sure, the corporate scandals we hear of likely make most people want to turn their back on capitalist systems. These events, and their reports, make us believe that it is an inherently flawed system.

While capitalism is not perfect, it's the best we know.

Pull back the curtain on many of these corrupt corporate events and you will likely find some form of cronyism. Favourable regulations blocking others from entering the market. Tax incentives to certain companies make it an unfair playing field for smaller firms. Or government hand-outs to certain players whose failing institutions don't serve their end users well.

Progress and degrowth

In recent years the challenges of climate change have inevitably found their way into considerations about the future of capitalism.

The general argument today is that capitalism, with its focus on growth, is an unsuitable structure for the future – certainly a green one.

Instead, the cry goes out that the new world needs a new system, often accompanied by the phrase *degrowth*.

This idea should cause our hair to stand on end and raise more than a few concerns.

For one, we should question the assumptions being made.[158] Many of its proponents hold an outdated view of capitalism – overlooking the flexibility of this structure and confusing the *production method* with the structure of the business itself.

Making this mistake leads many to view *capitalism* and *mass production* as synonymous.

But, as we've looked at in this book, mass production was simply a technological method of the 1900s.

Tomorrow's technological breakthrough will be very different but will be just as fervently adopted by businesses, as has been the case at every turning of the innovation cycle. Companies that fail to keep up, fail.

Each time there is a paradigm shift, the underlying technology shifts too. It is the strength, not the weakness, of capitalism as a system that can adapt to each new paradigm.

The businesses that best harness the technology of the day rise to the top. One hundred years ago, the leading technology was found in steel, oil, and mass production. Firms such as Bethlehem steel were unsurprisingly the largest in the world at the time.

Today the leading technology has changed – and firms that harness the power of the semi-conductor are the world's biggest. Companies such as Microsoft, Alphabet, and Amazon.

The next era of paradigm-shifting technological change, which I suggest is just around the corner, could disrupt this leader board again. This is almost guaranteed if *these* leading firms fail to adapt to the new production method.

Separating these two points is important: the technology employed in the economy is separate from the economy's structure.

The key mistake degrowthers make is they see little progress. They miss the fundamental shifts that occur due to innovation cycles.

They overlook that our consumption patterns, desires, and wants have changed many times – and are set to change again.

As we've looked at, the capitalist economy centres itself around a reward system that highly favours those that best meet the needs of society.

Consumers earn money and then use it like a real-time voting machine. The companies that best solve consumers' needs receive the most votes – or in this case, money.

The degrowth group typically overlooks the human good of people, and how changes in consumer attitudes directly bring change in the economy.

Instead, like the socialist and communist shouts of past eras, degrowthers state that the people don't know what's good for them, they need leaders (normally the same people proclaiming this) that have far better insight and can – if given a little more power – make all their problems disappear.

While persuasive and enticing, these are, unfortunately, hollow arguments and promises.

The very idea of decoupling growth and innovation – and only keeping the innovation – is a dangerous one. It overlooks basic tenants of human motivation, risk-taking, and reward.

While some countries in history have managed to 'inspire' work without reward, it is often replaced with threat, punishment, and violence.

Degrowthers likely believe that their theories have real merit. In their minds, and according to their models, it could work.

But innovation is not reducible to a formula. It's about people striving to overcome issues and taking risks to combine ideas that no one ever thought of.

Those things happen less frequently in sterile environments. In fact, innovation has a lot to do with allowing failure.

The idea of a steady-state economy that controls growth and retains innovation speaks of the illusion that change is calm, steady, and constant. As we've looked at, change and innovation isn't any of these things.

Controlled economies fail to make these all-important jumps in growth and innovation simply because they are striving for stability. As a result, they typically decline into poverty and human hardship repeatedly because they have cut off the very thing that brought about progress. They miss the system's complexity and mistakenly think of it as something far simpler.

The calls from those in policy circles eye the ideas of degrowth and the need for policy to step in and better control the economy to help save the planet. It's alluring, and I am sure it is with well-meaning intentions. Their vision of degrowth sees it necessary for governments to become far more intervening, with far increased measures of direct controls, new taxes, new caps, and regulations of how and what is produced.

In doing so, they are likely to kill the goose that laid the golden egg.

Capitalism and a democratic society are key to the innovation waves we have seen in the past, and that we require in the future.

It is a complex system, and you cannot simply step in and remove economic growth from innovation. The two are linked.

In fact, the profit mechanism is one of the core reasons entrepreneurs are willing to take risks to solve other people's issues – it brings the chance of growth and reward.

The products and services capitalism produces are in response to individuals' needs and wants. As these consumer needs change to greener, more environmentally conscious alternatives, companies will have to keep up, or close their doors.

The future green economy is far from incompatible with capitalism. Capitalism is a highly adaptable system.

Beyond this, it's the only system we know that brings together the collective wisdom, intelligence, and the creativity we need today to meet these challenges head-on. To spur on human progress across the board.

The biggest risk to the collective progress of humanity is not the issues we see up ahead, but the naive tearing down of the structures that brought us progress in the first place.

Conclusion

∞

We have covered a lot of ground in this book. We have looked at how innovation cycles, information revolutions, and megatrends can influence and converge to bring about change.

From where I stand, the innovation occurring today is incredible. Look back, and we see this as a core attribute of humanity – our remarkable ability to adapt and overcome.

Today, when we dig a little deeper, we find thousands of individuals and companies finding solutions to many of the issues we face.

We should never forget that innovation is not smooth but instead jumps at certain key points. This is how it has played out in each of the waves of innovation since the industrial revolution and the global orders before that.

We should strive to be more alert to change. Become more observant, remembering that the world that we see around us today is only a temporary state. It's only been like this for a short time, and it is already moving toward the next one.

We must encounter a paradox in seeing change at this scale.

We need to stand back, both metaphorically and cognitively. For all its amazing advancements, our modern world has made us far more short-term in our thinking. It has made us hyper-specialists in a very narrow field.

But to see global change, we have to broaden the vision that we use. We have to widen our lens and see how moving parts are connected. While this sounds challenging at first, the more you practice, the easier it becomes.

These trends and megatrends that I encourage you to look at operate at a far slower speed than our day-to-day lives. Their timescales can be measured in decades, not minutes. We, therefore, need to slow our thinking and change our perspective to best see them.

Over the years, there has been a story I share that helps people *get it.*

A few hundred meters away from my house, there's a bench. The bench itself is nothing special. It's simply a weather-battered wooden bench – the kind you find in most public spaces in the UK

But it's the location that makes it. High up above Llandudno, the view is incredible. You can watch the waves roll in from the town's west and east shores. Some days those two beaches can seem a million miles apart. Different world and weather systems. One calm, one rough.

The town, too. Even on its busiest days, its Victorian streets appear calm. Even orderly. At least from this elevated position.

Standing back brings new perspectives. It allows you to escape the noise and see things with more clarity.

We're used to doing this when it comes to landscapes, but less so when we approach less tangible things such as change and innovation.

Rarely do we give ourselves time to sit at the hypothetical bench and view things from this elevated vantage point.

But we should. It brings great perspectives.

It also gives us space – and a stillness – that allows curiosity to flourish.

Here's to your growing curiosity about the incredible world around you.

References

∞

[1] Horowitz, J. and Graf, N., 2022. *Most U.S. Teens See Anxiety and Depression as a Major Problem Among Their Peers.* [online] Pew Research Center's Social & Demographic Trends Project.
Available at: <https://www.pewresearch.org/social-trends/2019/02/20/most-u-s-teens-see-anxiety-and-depression-as-a-major-problem-among-their-peers/> [Accessed 10 March 2021].

[2] Goodwin, R., Weinberger, A., Kim, J., Wu, M. and Galea, S., 2020. Trends in anxiety among adults in the United States, 2008–2018: Rapid increases among young adults. Journal of Psychiatric Research, 130, pp.441-446.

[3] Dimock, M. and Wike, R., 2020. *America is exceptional in the nature of its political divide.* [online] Pew Research Center. Available at: <https://www.pewresearch.org/fact-tank/2020/11/13/america-is-exceptional-in-the-nature-of-its-political-divide/> [Accessed 7 May 2022].

[4] Bunyan, R., 2019. *18 Killed As Thousands of Protestors Take to the Streets in Chile. Here's What to Know.* [online] Time. Available at: <https://time.com/5710268/chile-protests/> [Accessed 7 May 2022].

[5] Bunyan, R., 2019. *18 Killed As Thousands of Protestors Take to the Streets in Chile. Here's What to Know*. [online] Time. Available at: <https://time.com/5710268/chile-protests/> [Accessed 7 May 2022].

[6] Anonymous, 2022. *Hong Kong is in danger. China's promise of democracy was a lie | Anonymous*. [online] the Guardian. Available at: <https://www.theguardian.com/commentisfree/2019/jun/13/lawyer-protesting-law-hong-kong-extradition-bill-china> [Accessed 10 January 2020].

[7] Lambert, M., 2022. *Miley Cyrus Has Finally Found Herself*. [online] ELLE. Available at: <https://www.elle.com/culture/music/a28280119/miley-cyrus-elle-interview/> [Accessed 12 January 2020].

[8] Katanich, D., 2022. *New York could be underwater by 2050. But the city has a plan*. [online] euronews. Available at: <https://www.euronews.com/green/2021/12/15/new-york-is-building-a-wall-to-combat-the-worst-effects-of-climate-change> [Accessed 18 January 2022].

[9] Bir, B., 2022. *Environmental disasters across globe in January 2022*. [online] Aa.com.tr. Available at: <https://www.aa.com.tr/en/environment/environmental-disasters-across-globe-in-january-2022/2501344> [Accessed 22 April 2022].

[10] Mecklin, J., 2022. *Current Time - 2022 - Bulletin of the Atomic Scientists*. [online] Bulletin of the Atomic Scientists. Available at: <https://thebulletin.org/doomsday-clock/current-time/> [Accessed 24 January 2022].

[11]Dixon, B., 1971. In Praise of Prophets. *New Scientist*, (51), p.606.

[12] Ehrlich, P., 1968. *The Population Bomb*. New York, NY: Ballantine Books.

[13] Pentland, W., 2011. *Thomas Malthus: Wrong Yesterday, Right Today?*. [online] Forbes.
Available at:
<https://www.forbes.com/sites/williampentland/2011/01/09/thomas-malthus-wrong-yesterday-right-today/?sh=5eacc9b24595> [Accessed 19 March 2021].

[14]RICHARDS, D. and HUNT, J., 1983. *An Illustrated History of Modern Britain, etc.* 3rd ed. Longman Group, p.7.

[15] Miceli, M. and Castelfranchi, C., 2015. *Expectancy & Emotion*. 1st ed. Oxford University Press, p.3.

[16] UK Parliament. n.d. *Enclosing the land*. [online] Available at: <https://www.parliament.uk/about/living-heritage/transformingsociety/towncountry/landscape/overview/enclosingland/> [Accessed 27 April 2022].

[17] UK Parliament. n.d. *Enclosing the land.* [online] Available at: <https://www.parliament.uk/about/living-heritage/transformingsociety/towncountry/landscape/overview/enclosingland/> [Accessed 27 April 2022].

[18] Lloyd, Amy J.: "Emigration, Immigration and Migration in Nineteenth Century Britain." British Library Newspapers. Detroit: Gale, 2007.

[19] Parry, Martin, Arnell, Nigel, McMichael, Tony, Nicholls, Robert, Martens, Pim, Kovats, Sari, Livermore, Matthew, Rosenzweig, Cynthia, Iglesias, Ana and Fischer, Gunther (2001) Millions at risk: defining critical climate change threats and targets. *Global Environmental Change*, 11 (3), 181-183. (doi:10.1016/S0959-3780(01)00011-5).

[20] Monbiot, G., 2006. *Heat.* London: Allen Lane, p.16.

[21] Tollefson, J., 2021. *COVID curbed carbon emissions in 2020 – but not by much.* [online] Nature.com. Available at: <https://www.nature.com/articles/d41586-021-00090-3> [Accessed 15 September 2021].

[22] Grinin, L. and Grinin, A., 2016. The Sixth Kondratieff Wave and the Cybernetic Revolution. *Globalistics and Globalization Studies*, pp.337-355.

[23] 2017. *Perils of Perception.* [online] Available at: <https://www.ipsos.com/en-uk/perils-perception-2017> [Accessed 4 January 2021].

[24] Wasson, D., 2022. *Commodus.* [online] World History Encyclopedia.
Available at:
<https://www.worldhistory.org/commodus/> [Accessed 12 November 2020].

[25] Dalby, A., 2002. *Empire of pleasures.* London: Routledge.

[26] Pliny and Rackham, H., 1940. *Natural history.* Harvard University Press.

[27] Hopkinsmedicine.org. n.d. *Do Sleep Trackers Really Work?.* [online]
Available at:
<https://www.hopkinsmedicine.org/health/wellness-and-prevention/do-sleep-trackers-really-work> [Accessed 22 December 2021].

[28] Hirshkowitz, M., Whiton, K., Albert, S. M., Alessi, C., Bruni, O., DonCarlos, L., Hazen, N., Herman, J., Katz, E. S., Kheirandish-Gozal, L., Neubauer, D. N., O'Donnell, A. E., Ohayon, M., Peever, J., Rawding, R., Sachdeva, R. C., Setters, B., Vitiello, M. V., Ware, J. C., & Adams Hillard, P. J. (2015). National Sleep Foundation's sleep time duration recommendations: Methodology and results summary. *Sleep Health, 1*(1), 40–43.
https://doi.org/10.1016/j.sleh.2014.12.010

[29] Ekirch, A., 2006. *At Day's Close: Night in Times Past.* W. W. Norton & Company.

[30] Freeman, M., 2002. *Human rights*. Cambridge, UK: Polity Press.

[31] Hooper, F., 1980. *Roman realities*. Detroit: Wayne State University Press.

[32] Hrlibrary.umn.edu. n.d. *A Short History of Human Rights*. [online]
Available at:
<http://hrlibrary.umn.edu/edumat/hreduseries/hereandnow/Part-1/short-history.htm> [Accessed 6 July 2021].

[33] Le Roy Ladurie, E., 1971. *Times of feast, times of famine*. Garden City, N.J: Doubleday.

[34] Historyextra.com. 2022. *The Strangest Causes of Death in the Medieval Period | History Extra*. [online]
Available at:
<https://www.historyextra.com/period/medieval/strange-causes-death-medieval-period-how-did-they-die/>
[Accessed 17 August 2021].

[35] Durn, S., 2021. *Medieval elites used handwashing as a shrewd 'power play.' Here's how.*. [online] National Geographic.
Available at:
<https://www.nationalgeographic.com/history/article/medieval-elites-used-handwashing-as-shrewd-power-play>
[Accessed 22 December 2021].

[36] Kannadan, A., 2018. History of the Miasma Theory of Disease. *ESSAI*, 16(18).

[37] Hugill, P., 2004. *World trade since 1431*. Baltimore, Md: The Johns Hopkins Univ. Press.

[38] Britishwaterways.co.uk. 2011. [online] Available at: <http://www.britishwaterways.co.uk/media/documents/publications/British-Waterways-Annual-Report-and-Accounts-2011-12.pdf> [Accessed 13 February 2022].

[39] Max Roser, Hannah Ritchie and Bernadeta Dadonaite (2013) - "Child and Infant Mortality". Published online at OurWorldInData.org.
Retrieved from: 'https://ourworldindata.org/child-mortality' [Online Resource]

[40] Peters, A., McEwen, B. and Friston, K., 2017. Uncertainty and stress: Why it causes diseases and how it is mastered by the brain. *Progress in Neurobiology*, 156, pp.164-188.

[41] https://www.wellesnet.com/the-war-of-the-worlds-radio-script/

[42] Bento, A., Nguyen, T., Wing, C., Lozano-Rojas, F., Ahn, Y. and Simon, K., 2020. Evidence from internet search data shows information-seeking responses to news of local COVID-19 cases. *Proceedings of the National Academy of Sciences*, 117(21), pp.11220-11222.

[43] Buchanan K, Aknin LB, Lotun S, Sandstrom GM (2021) Brief exposure to social media during the COVID-19 pandemic: Doom-scrolling has negative emotional consequences, but kindness-scrolling does not. PLoS ONE 16(10): e0257728.
https://doi.org/10.1371/journal.pone.0257728

[44] Peters, A., McEwen, B. and Friston, K., 2017. Uncertainty and stress: Why it causes diseases and how it is mastered by the brain. *Progress in Neurobiology*, 156, pp.164-188.

[45] Ramirez, A., & Arbuckle, M. R. (2016). Synaptic Plasticity: The Role of Learning and Unlearning in Addiction and Beyond. Biological psychiatry, 80(9), e73–e75. https://doi.org/10.1016/j.biopsych.2016.09.002

[46] McEwen B. S. (2006). Protective and damaging effects of stress mediators: central role of the brain. Dialogues in clinical neuroscience, 8(4), 367–381. https://doi.org/10.31887/DCNS.2006.8.4/bmcewen

[47] McEwen BS. Physiology and neurobiology of stress and adaptation: central role of the brain. Physiol Rev. 2007 Jul;87(3):873-904. doi: 10.1152/physrev.00041.2006. PMID: 17615391.

[48] European Commission, 2007. *European Economy Economic Forecast Autumn 2007*. European Commission.

[49] Steve Keen, "Mad, bad and dangerous to know ", real-world economics review, issue no. 49, 12 March 2009, pp. 2-7, http://www.paecon.net/PAEReview/issue49/Keen49.pdf

[50] Hudson.org. 2022. *Events - Vice President Mike Pence's Remarks on the Administration's Policy Towards China - October - 2018 - Hudson Institute.* [online] Available at: <https://www.hudson.org/events/1610-vice-president-mike-pence-s-remarks-on-the-administration-s-policy-towards-china102018> [Accessed 10 April 2019].

[51] Li, C., 2016. *Assessing U.S.-China relations under the Obama administration.* [online] Brookings.edu. Available at: <https://www.brookings.edu/opinions/assessing-u-s-china-relations-under-the-obama-administration/> [Accessed 17 February 2020].

[52] Lowy Institute, 2021. *Asia Power Index 2021.* [online] Available at: <https://power.lowyinstitute.org/> [Accessed 15 November 2021].

[53] Ipss.go.jp. n.d. *National Institute of Population and Social Security Research.* [online] Available at: <https://www.ipss.go.jp/index-e.asp> [Accessed 9 October 2021].

[54] Meola, 2022, Future demand for elderly care services like assisted living & in-home care are rife for digital disruption. Business Insider.
https://www.businessinsider.com/senior-care-market-trends?r=US&IR=T

[55] Dong & Ding, 2009. Aging in China: a challenge or opportunity?
https://pubmed.ncbi.nlm.nih.gov/19716060/

[56] Zhai, 2017, The Impacts of the Universal Two-Child Policy on China's Population.
https://link.springer.com/article/10.1007/BF03500915

[57] Feldstein, 2006, The Effect of Taxes on Efficiency and Growth, National Bureau of Economic Research.
https://www.nber.org/papers/w12201

[58] Fergnani, A., 2020. Corporate foresight: A new frontier for strategy and management. *Academy of Management Perspectives*.

[59] Pyper, J., 2013. *Has the U.S. Love of the Automobile Peaked?*. [online] Scientific American. Available at: <https://www.scientificamerican.com/article/has-the-us-love-of-the-automobile-peaked/> [Accessed 21 October 2021].

[60] Bts.gov. 2021. *Number of U.S. Aircraft, Vehicles, Vessels, and Other Conveyances | Bureau of Transportation Statistics.* [online] Available at: <https://www.bts.gov/content/number-us-aircraft-vehicles-vessels-and-other-conveyances> [Accessed 30 July 2021].

[61] Sivak, M., 2013. *HAS MOTORIZATION IN THE U.S. PEAKED?.* The University of Michigan Transportation Research Institute.

[62]Chatterjee, K., Goodwin, P., Schwanen, T., Clark, B., Jain, J., Melia, S., Middleton, J., Plyushteva, A., Ricci, M., Santos, G. and Stokes, G. (2018). Young People's Travel – What's Changed and Why? Review and Analysis. Report to Department for Transport. UWE Bristol, UK. www.gov.uk/government/publications/young-peoples-travel-whats-changed-andwhy

[63] Pittenger, C., Duman, R. Stress, Depression, and Neuroplasticity: A Convergence of Mechanisms. Neuropsychopharmacol 33, 88–109 (2008). https://doi.org/10.1038/sj.npp.1301574

[64]
https://www.ncbi.nlm.nih.gov/pmc/articles/PMC3548359/

[65] McKinsey Global Institute, 2017. *Jobs Lost, Jobs Gained: workforce transitions in a time of automation.* McKinsey & Company.

[66] Garside, M., 2020. *UK coal industry employment 1920-2019 | Statista.* [online] Statista. Available at: <https://www.statista.com/statistics/371069/employment-in-coal-mining-industry-in-the-united-kingdom-uk/> [Accessed 16 March 2021].

[67] Fothergill, S., n.d. *THE UK's TRANSITION FROM COAL.* [online] Eesc.europa.eu. Available at: <https://www.eesc.europa.eu/sites/default/files/files/fothergill.pdf> [Accessed 18 February 2022].

[68] LaFrance, A., 2015. *17 of the Best Internet Reactions to the Original iPhone.* [online] The Atlantic. Available at: <https://www.theatlantic.com/technology/archive/2015/11/17-of-the-best-internet-reactions-to-the-original-iphone/415095/> [Accessed 22 April 2022].

[69] Norcross JC, Vangarelli DJ. The resolution solution: longitudinal examination of New Year's change attempts. J Subst Abuse. 1988-1989;1(2):127-34. doi: 10.1016/s0899-3289(88)80016-6. PMID: 2980864.

[70]

https://www.neuroscience.lu.se/sites/neuroscience.lu.se/files/the_discovery_of_dopamine_pdf.pdf

[71] Georgia Health Sciences University. "Habit formation is enabled by gateway to brain cells." ScienceDaily. ScienceDaily, 13 January 2012. <www.sciencedaily.com/releases/2011/12/111221140448.htm>.

[72] Drjimtaylor.com

[73] Federal Reserve Board, Washington, D.C., 2007. Anchoring Bias in Consensus Forecasts and its Effect on Market Prices.

[74] Cherry, K., 2022. The Recency Effect in Psychology. [online] verywellmind.com. Available at: <https://www.verywellmind.com/the-recency-effect-4685058#:~:text=items%20are%20recalled.-,Overview,the%20item%20on%20that%20list.&text=The%20recency%20effect%20can%20tell%20us%20a%20bit%20about%20how%20memory%20works.> [Accessed 2 April 2022].

[75] Blum, S. Failure to Perceive Change: From Neurons to Social Networks. *Hu Arenas* (2021). https://doi.org/10.1007/s42087-020-00180-0

[76] Schopenhauer, A. (1907). The World as Will and Idea (6th ed.). Kegan Paul, Trench, Trubner & Co Ltd.

[77] Koltko-Rivera, M. (2004). The Psychology of Worldviews. *Review of General Psychology*, *8*(1), 3–58.
[78] McLeod, S. (2020). Thomas Kuhn - Science as a Paradigm. Simple Psychology. https://www.simplypsychology.org/Kuhn-Paradigm.html

[79] Chapter 3: The guy who started talking about greenhouse gases causing climate change in the 1800s

[80] Max Planck, Scientific autobiography, 1950

[81] https://en.wikipedia.org/wiki/Timeline_of_the_telephone

[82] https://www.jstor.org/stable/24913627

[83] Dupont, Keeling, Weiss, 2016, First Cabin Fare from New York to the British Isles 1826 -1914, NBER Working Paper. https://www.nber.org/system/files/working_papers/w22426/w22426.pdf

[84] https://www.businessinsider.com/retail-courts-gen-z-spending-power-over-140-billion-2020-1?IR=T

[85]https://www.mckinsey.com/~/media/McKinsey/Industries/Consumer%20Packaged%20Goods/Our%20Insights/True%20Gen%20Generation%20Z%20and%20its%20implications%20for%20companies/Generation-Z-and-its-implication-for-companies.pdf

[86] Scheier M. F., Carver, C. S., & Bridges, M. W. (2001). Optimism, pessimism, and psychological well-being. In Chang E. (Ed.), *Optimism & Pessimism: Implications for theory, research, and practice* (pp. 189-216). American Psychological Association.

[87] Lee, L. O., James, P., Zevon, E. S., Kim, E. S., Trudel-Fitzgerald, C., Spiro, A., Grodstein, F., & Kubzansky, L. D. (2019). Optimism is associated with exceptional longevity in 2 epidemiologic cohorts of men and women. *Proceedings of the National Academy of Sciences, 116*(37), 18357–18362.

[88] Proffitt, S. (1999, January 24). Martin Seligman: Pursuing happiness with a positive outlook, not a pill. *Los Angeles Times.* https://www.latimes.com/archives/la-xpm-1999-jan-24-op-1083-story.html

[89] McAfee, D., Doubleday, Z. A., Geiger, N., & Connell, S. D. (2019). Everyone loves a success story: Optimism inspires conservation engagement. *BioScience, 69*(4), 274–281.

[90] Petersen, A. R. (2015). *Hope in health : the socio-politics of optimism.* Palgrave Macmillan.

[91] Branson, R. (2020, October 1). *Simon Sinek on the difference between positive and optimistic.* Virgin. https://www.virgin.com/branson-family/richard-branson-blog/simon-sinek-on-the-difference-between-positive-and-optimistic

[92] Housel, M. (2018, July 18). *Mindsets: Optimism vs. Complacency vs. Pessimism.* Collaborative Fund. https://www.collaborativefund.com/blog/mindsets-optimism-vs-complacency-vs-pessimism/

[93] Scheier M. F., Carver, C. S., & Bridges, M. W. (2001). Optimism, pessimism, and psychological well-being. In Chang E. (Ed.), *Optimism & Pessimism: Implications for theory, research, and practice* (pp. 189-216). American Psychological Association.

[94] Rand, K. L., Shanahan, M. L., Fischer, I. C., & Fortney, S. K. (2020). Hope and optimism as predictors of academic performance and subjective well-being in college students. *Learning and Individual Differences, 81*, 101906.

[95] Arslan, G., & Yıldırım, M. (2021). Coronavirus stress, meaningful living, optimism, and depressive symptoms: a study of moderated mediation model. *Australian Journal of Psychology, 73*(2), 113-124.

[96] Conversano, C., Rotondo, A., Lensi, E., Vista, O. D., Arpone, F., & Reda, M. A. (2010). Optimism and its impact on mental and physical well-being. *Clinical Practice & Epidemiology in Mental Health, 1*(1), 25–29. Gillham, J. E., Shatté, A. J., Reivich, K. J, & Seligman, M. E. (2001). Optimism, pessimism, and explanatory style. In Chang E. (Ed.), *Optimism & Pessimism: Implications for theory, research, and practice* (pp. 53-75). American Psychological Association.

[97] Chamuah, A., & Sankar, R. (2018). Resilience, learned optimism and self esteem as predictors of psychological well being. *International Journal Of All Research Writings, 1*(5), 1-4.

[98] Petersen, A. R. (2015). *Hope in health : the socio-politics of optimism*. Palgrave Macmillan.

[99] Morton, S., Mergler, A., & Boman, P. (2013). Managing the transition: The role of optimism and self-efficacy for first-year Australian university students. *Journal of Psychologists and Counsellors in Schools, 24*(1), 90-108.

[100] Rasmussen, H. N., & Wallio, S. C. (2008). The Health Benefits of Optimism. In Lopez Shane (Ed.), *Positive psychology: Exploring the best in people, Vol 2: Capitalizing on emotional experiences* (pp. 131–150). Praeger Publishers.

[101] Rand, K. L., Shanahan, M. L., Fischer, I. C., & Fortney, S. K. (2020). Hope and optimism as predictors of academic performance and subjective well-being in college students. *Learning and Individual Differences, 81*, 101906.

[102] Morton, S., Mergler, A., & Boman, P. (2013). Managing the transition: The role of optimism and self-efficacy for first-year Australian university students. *Journal of Psychologists and Counsellors in Schools, 24*(1), 90-108.

[103] Morton, S., Mergler, A., & Boman, P. (2013). Managing the transition: The role of optimism and self-efficacy for first-year Australian university students. *Journal of Psychologists and Counsellors in Schools, 24*(1), 90-108.

[104] Arslan, G., & Yıldırım, M. (2021). Coronavirus stress, meaningful living, optimism, and depressive symptoms: a study of moderated mediation model. *Australian Journal of Psychology, 73*(2), 113-124.

[105] Conversano, C., Rotondo, A., Lensi, E., Vista, O. D., Arpone, F., & Reda, M. A. (2010). Optimism and its impact on mental and physical well-being. *Clinical Practice & Epidemiology in Mental Health, 1*(1), 25–29. Gillham, J. E., Shatté, A. J., Reivich, K. J, & Seligman, M. E. (2001). Optimism, pessimism, and explanatory style. In Chang E. (Ed.), *Optimism & Pessimism: Implications for theory, research, and practice* (pp. 53-75). American Psychological Association.

[106] McAfee, D., Doubleday, Z. A., Geiger, N., & Connell, S. D. (2019). Everyone loves a success story: Optimism inspires conservation engagement. *BioScience, 69*(4), 274–281.

[107] Terrill, A. L., Ruiz, J. M., & Garofalo, J. P. (2010). Look on the bright side: do the benefits of optimism depend on the social nature of the stressor? *Journal of Behavioral Medicine, 33*(5), 399–414.

[108] Seligman, M. E. (1991). Learned optimism: how to change your mind and your life. Pocket Books.

[109] Scheier M. F., Carver, C. S., & Bridges, M. W. (2001). Optimism, pessimism, and psychological well-being. In Chang E. (Ed.), *Optimism & Pessimism: Implications for theory, research, and practice* (pp. 189-216). American Psychological Association.

[110] Petersen, A. R. (2015). *Hope in health : the socio-politics of optimism*. Palgrave Macmillan.

[111] McAfee, D., Doubleday, Z. A., Geiger, N., & Connell, S. D. (2019). Everyone loves a success story: Optimism inspires conservation engagement. *BioScience, 69*(4), 274–281.

[112] Statista. 2021. *Global marketing data market size 2021 | Statista.* [online] Available at: <https://www.statista.com/statistics/818754/global-marketing-data-market-size/> [Accessed 7 May 2022].

[113] *Georg Simmel.* (n.d.). Good Reads. Retrieved October 20, 2021, from https://www.goodreads.com/author/show/68201.Georg_Simmel

[114] Simon, H. (1971). *Designing organizations for an information rich world.* Computers, communications, and the public interest, Baltimore.

[115] Schenk, M. (1997). *A Small Dark Place by Martin Schenk (1997–10-07)* (1st ed.). Villard.

[116] Oppenheim, C (1997) Managers' use and handling of information. International Journal of Information Management 17(4): 246.

[117] Edmunds, A., & Morris, A. (2000). The problem of information overload in business organisations: a review of the literature. *International Journal of Information Management, 20*, 17–28.

[118] *Meadows, D. (1998). Indicators and Information Systems for Sustainable Development. Hartland/VT: Sustainability Institute.*

[119] Levitin, D. (2014). *The organized mind: Thinking straight in the age of information overload.* Penguin Books.

[120] Simon, H., & Newell, A. (1971). *Human problem solving: The state of the theory in 1970.* American Psychologist. https://www.semanticscholar.org/paper/Human-problem-solving%3A-The-state-of-the-theory-in-Simon-Newell/18ce82b07ac84aaf30b502c93076cec2accbfcaa

[121] https://www.aaii.com/sentimentsurvey

[122]https://www.pewresearch.org/fact-tank/2020/04/01/more-than-nine-in-ten-people-worldwide-live-in-countries-with-travel-restrictions-amid-covid-19/

[123] https://pubmed.ncbi.nlm.nih.gov/9599441/

[124] Blex, C. (2020, October 23). *How social media echo chambers emerge (and why all your friends think Trump will lose).* Oxford Internet Institute. https://www.oii.ox.ac.uk/blog/how-social-media-echo-chambers-emerge-and-why-all-your-friends-think-trump-will-lose/

[125] Robson, D. (2018, April 17). *The myth of the online echo chamber.* Future. https://www.bbc.com/future/article/20180416-the-myth-of-the-online-echo-chamber

[126] Cota, W., Ferriera, S., Pastor-Satorras, R., & Starnini, M. (2019, December 9). *Quantifying echo chamber effects in information spreading over political communication networks.* Springer Open. https://epjdatascience.springeropen.com/articles/10.1140/epjds/s13688-019-0213-9

[127] *How Filter Bubbles Distort Reality: Everything You Need to Know.* (n.d.). Farnam Street. Retrieved 2021, from https://fs.blog/2017/07/filter-bubbles/

[128] *Measuring the "Filter Bubble": How Google is influencing what you click.* (2018, December 4). DuckDuckGo. https://spreadprivacy.com/google-filter-bubble-study/

[129] Webber, E. (2017, February 11). *A brief introduction to groupthink, homogeneity and echo chambers.* Emily Webber. https://emilywebber.co.uk/avoiding-groupthink-echo-chambers-diversity-multidisciplinary-team-short-talk/

[130] *GROUPTHINK.* (2013, October 21). David Zahra & Associates. https://www.davidzahra.com/resources/blogs/groupthink/

[131] *Asch conformity experiments.* (n.d.). Wikipedia. Retrieved 2021, from https://en.wikipedia.org/wiki/Asch_conformity_experiments

[132] Hitler, A. (1925). *Mein Kampf* (1st ed.). Franz Eher Nachfolger GmbH.

[133] Stratigakos, D. (2019, November 6). *The Invasion of Memory: Hitler's Attempt to Rewrite the History of World War I.* THE JOURNAL OF THE AMERICAN INSTITUTE OF ARCHITECTS. https://www.architectmagazine.com/design/culture/the-invasion-of-memory-hitlers-attempt-to-rewrite-the-history-of-world-war-i_o

[134] Holiday, R. (2014, February 26). *Outrage Porn: How the Need For "Perpetual Indignation" Manufactures Phony Offense.* Observer. https://observer.com/2014/02/outrage-porn-how-the-need-for-perpetual-indignation-manufactures-phony-offense/

[135] Perlmutter, A. (2019, September 19). *How Negative News Distorts Our Thinking.* Psychology Today. https://www.psychologytoday.com/gb/blog/the-modern-brain/201909/how-negative-news-distorts-our-thinking

[136] Stafford, T. (2017, January 31). *How to get people to overcome their bias.* BBC. https://www.bbc.com/future/article/20170131-why-wont-some-people-listen-to-reason

[137] Marx, Sabine M. and Weber, Elke U., Decision Making Under Climate Uncertainty: The Power of Understanding Judgment and Decision Processes (2012). In T. Dietz & D.C. Bidwell (Eds.), Climate change in the Great Lakes region: Navigating an Uncertain Future. East Lansing, MI: Michigan State University Press. Forthcoming, Columbia

Business School Research Paper No. 13-59, Available at SSRN: https://ssrn.com/abstract=2293125

[138] Schirrmeister, E., Gohring, A., & Warnke, P. (2020, February 3). *Psychological biases and heuristics in the context of foresight and scenario processes.* Wiley Online Library. https://onlinelibrary.wiley.com/doi/10.1002/ffo2.31

[139] Schirrmeister, E., Gohring, A., & Warnke, P. (2020, February 3). *Psychological biases and heuristics in the context of foresight and scenario processes.* Wiley Online Library. https://onlinelibrary.wiley.com/doi/10.1002/ffo2.31

[140] Bechara A, Damasio AR, Damasio H, Anderson SW. Insensitivity to future consequences following damage to human prefrontal cortex. Cognition. 1994 Apr-Jun;50(1-3):7-15. doi: 10.1016/0010-0277(94)90018-3. PMID: 8039375.

[141] Armstrong & Graefe, 2010, Predicting Elections from the most important issue: A test of the Take-the-best Heuristic.
https://repository.upenn.edu/cgi/viewcontent.cgi?article=1157&context=marketing_papers

[142] Gigerenzer, 2019, Expert Intuition is Not Rational Choice, American Journal of Psychology. https://doi.org/10.5406/amerjpsyc.132.4.0475

[143] Ericsson, K. A., Krampe, R. T., & Tesch-Römer, C. (1993). The role of deliberate practice in the acquisition of expert performance. *Psychological Review, 100*(3), 363–406. https://doi.org/10.1037/0033-295X.100.3.363

[144] Higgs, R., 2007. *If Men Were Angels: The Basic Analytics Of The State Versus Self-Government.* [online] Cdn.mises.org. Available at: <https://cdn.mises.org/21_4_7.pdf> [Accessed 7 May 2022].

[145] Aksoy et al, 2021, Calamities, Common Interests, Shared Identity: What shapes altruism and reciprocity? https://www.ucl.ac.uk/~uctpcab/research/EU_survey.pdf

[146] https://worldjusticeproject.org/sites/default/files/documents/WJP%20Insights%202020%20-%20Online%20.pdf

[147] Wolff, E., 2010. *Recent Trends in Household Wealth in the United States: Rising Debt and the Middle-Class Squeeze–an Update to 2007*. Working Paper No. 589. [online] Levy Economics Institute of Bard College. Available at: <https://www.levyinstitute.org/pubs/wp_589.pdf> [Accessed 7 May 2022].

[148] https://www.ft.com/content/0cf55624-5d0f-11e3-a558-00144feabdc0

[149] Muller, J., 2013. *Capitalism and Inequality.* [online] Foreign Affairs. Available at: <https://www.foreignaffairs.com/articles/2013-02-11/capitalism-and-inequality> [Accessed 7 May 2022].

[150] Robb, G., n.d. *The discovery of France*. Picador.

[151] Early, J., 2018. [online] Cato.org. Available at: <https://www.cato.org/policy-analysis/reassessing-facts-about-inequality-poverty-redistribution> [Accessed 7 May 2022].

[152] Perry, M., 2014. *Adjusting for transfers and taxes reduces income inequality between highest and lowest quintiles by 50%.* [online] AEI.org. Available at: <https://www.aei.org/carpe-diem/adjusting-transfers-federal-taxes-reduces-income-inequality-50/> [Accessed 7 May 2022].

[153] Almås, I. and Mogstad, M., 2011. Older or Wealthier? The Impact of Age Adjustment on Wealth Inequality*. *The Scandinavian Journal of Economics*, 114(1), pp.24-54.

[154] 2008, Gabaix & Landier, Why has CEO pay increased so much? Quarterly Journal of Economics: http://pages.stern.nyu.edu/~xgabaix/papers/ceoPay.pdf

[155] Edmans, A., n.d. *Why has CEO pay risen so much faster than worker pay? - Alex Edmans.* [online] Alex Edmans. Available at: <https://alexedmans.com/blog/executive-pay/why-has-ceo-pay-risen-so-much-faster-than-worker-pay/#:~:text=Suddenly%2C%20his%20%2410%20million%20salary,rise%20when%20firm%20size%20rises.> [Accessed 7 May 2022].

[156] Bianco, M. and Martini, C., 2021. *'We get by day to day': Argentina's high poverty rate dips as pandemic eases.* [online] Reuters.com. Available at: <https://www.reuters.com/world/americas/we-live-day-day-almost-half-argentines-shadow-poverty-2021-09-30/> [Accessed 7 May 2022].

[157] A Meltzer, 2012. Why Capitalism?

[158] Mastini, R., 2017. *Degrowth: the case for a new economic paradigm.* [online] https://www.opendemocracy.net/. Available at: <https://www.opendemocracy.net/en/degrowth-case-for-constructing-new-economic-paradigm/> [Accessed 7 May 2022].

[ii] Winning the Nobel Prize for Chemistry in 1903

Printed in Great Britain
by Amazon

26219876R00189